VOLUME 2

Stories Behind

50
Southern Gospel
Favorites

VOLUME 2

Stories Behind

50

Southern Gospel Favorites

Lindsay Terry

FOREWORD BY MOSIE LISTER

Kregel
Publications

Stories Behind 50 Southern Gospel Favorites, Volume 2

© 2005 by Lindsay Terry

Published by Kregel Publications, a division of Kregel, Inc., P.O. Box 2607, Grand Rapids, MI 49501.

Unless otherwise indicated, Scripture quotations are from the King James Version of the Holy Bible.

Cover photograph © Paul Wharton Photography

Library of Congress Cataloging-in-Publication Data
Stories behind 50 southern gospel favorites, volume 2
/ by Lindsay Terry.
    p.   cm.
Includes bibliographical references and index.
    1. Hymns, English—History and criticism. I. Title:
Stories behind fifty southern gospel favorites. II. Title.
BV315 .T46   2002   264'.23—dc21
2002011859

ISBN 0-8254-3885-3

Printed in the United States of America

05 06 07 08 09 / 5 4 3 2 1

To the adult choir of Crescent Beach Baptist Church, Crescent Beach, Florida (near St. Augustine), whose enthusiasm and faithfulness is commendable indeed. I salute their sincere desire to make their music the best that it can be for the greater glory of our Savior. I particularly want to express my appreciation for one of the bass singers, and the cheerleader of the group, Mr. Jack Bland.

Contents

CONTENTS

Part 2: A Special Section of Classic Hymns and Gospel Songs Often Recorded and Performed by Southern Gospel Groups

Foreword

$\mathcal{F}$or many years the Lord has allowed me to be involved with the wonderful ministry of Southern Gospel Music. I have had the privilege of writing songs that have been sung and recorded by thousands of Southern Gospel Music groups. I have also had the opportunity to sing with at least one legendary quartet, the Statesmen, when we had the joy of introducing Southern Gospel songs that went on to become standards, loved by Christians across our nation. It is interesting to know that these musical offerings came from the hearts of songwriters who were inspired to put on paper what the Lord was revealing to them at the time.

It is comforting to know that many of the songwriters whose stories appear in this book are people with fears and fantasies, problems and pleasures, and tears and triumphs, much the same as you and I. Out of these life experiences, God has given songs that have ministered to the hearts of Christians the world over. I am delighted that Lindsay has also included some of my stories in this book, as well as in volume one. I shared my first story with Lindsay as he visited in my home more than forty years ago in Tampa, Florida. We have remained friends since that time.

Through the stories included in this volume, you will "see the hearts" of the writers and read of the circumstances through which these songs came into being—songs such as "One Day at a Time," "He Came to Me," "Goodby, World, Goodby," or "High and Lifted Up," just to name a few. Second best to knowing the author of a song personally is being "introduced" to him or her through the printed page. I have had a "front-row seat" as I watched God move in the lives of many of these beloved songwriters, and yet my heart was lifted and refreshed once again as I read their stories.

All of the songs written about in this volume are favorites, and they will no doubt be even more meaningful to you after you understand how they came to life. After reading this book, as you sing or hear these musical creations, you can put names with them—not the names of the singers who made them famous but of the authors who gave them birth. Get to know them through this unique book—volume two of the series.

—MOSIE LISTER

Preface

For many years, as a music director and worship leader, I have had the privilege of telling the stories behind favorite songs to congregations that seem to hang on every word, not as a result of my ability to tell stories but because the stories are filled with human interest and excitement. I have often thought that if people love to hear the stories as they are told, then surely they would enjoy a book filled with these exciting stories—the stories behind their favorite Southern Gospel songs.

This book can be used for family or private devotional times, sermon illustrations, Sunday school lesson illustrations, or can be read to a group of children.

I have found that many, if not most, of the songs were born out of life's trials—sometimes severe testing and other times mild displeasure. Suddenly, from gloom springs glory. From the shadows comes a sunbeam—a song!

In interviews and conversations with these wonderful songwriters, I have been fortunate to get their stories. Without exception, each songwriter wanted his or her story told. They all wanted to share the circumstances surrounding the births of their songs. Although several of the songwriters have gone on to glory, I was able to get their stories through research.

May these stories allow you to "see" the hearts of this wonderful group of people.

Acknowledgments

Without the cooperation of the songwriters in giving their stories, this book would not be possible. Each of them was enthusiastic about sharing the details of the birth of their songs. It was refreshing to hear them giving God the glory for His gifts of the songs. I am grateful to each of them.

Thanks to Mosie Lister, whose foreword greatly adds to the effect of this volume. He is one of the most influential Southern Gospel songwriters of all time and has been a trusted friend for more than forty years.

Thanks also to Gary McSpadden who wrote a very helpful introduction to this book. For many years he has been a key person in the genre of Southern Gospel Music, as a singer, songwriter, producer, promoter, and emcee.

I am grateful to the people of Kregel Publications, especially to Jim Weaver for carrying the ball in getting volume one before the right people at Kregel, which led to this sequel. Janyre Tromp has faithfully overseen the details of getting volume two into the lineup of books to be published by Kregel. Her help with the promotion of volume one has been invaluable.

Becky Terry, my daughter-in-law and a court reporter who has taken a break to raise three wonderful little girls, did mountains of transcribing of the taped interviews on her equipment at home.

My wife, Marilyn, proofread the stories as they came from my computer, making very valuable suggestions as to how the stories could be told with greater effectiveness, rendering them more readable and interesting.

I appreciate the work of Belinda Flores and Lisa Kerr for their computer work, which was a great help in the completion of this book.

My appreciation to Gloria Gaither for furnishing information concerning the song "Because He Lives," taken from her book *Fully Alive* (copyright © 1964 by Gloria Gaither), published by Gaither Music Company.

Introduction

Gospel songs have been a part of my life for as long as I can remember. When I was three years old, my dad stood me on a chair and I sang a gospel song. When I was an older child, I sang gospel songs. When I was a teenager, I sang gospel songs. Today, I am still singing gospel songs. They have been a major part of the fabric of my life. What are the stories behind these wonderful songs and how did each one get from the writer's heart and mind to the listener's ear? Well, that is what this book is all about.

I went to my first Southern Gospel Music concert when I was nine years old, and I was hooked! The Blackwood Brothers and the Statesmen sang like I had never heard anyone sing before. They sang some of the Southern Gospel songs I had already learned to love. In the days of my life that have followed that concert, I have seen those great gospel songs touch and change the lives of countless numbers of people.

While I was singing with the Statesmen, the Oak Ridge Boys, the Imperials, the Bill Gaither Trio, the Gaither Vocal Band, or as a soloist, we always looked for "*the* song" when it was time to record a new project. We were looking for music and lyrics that would make a difference in someone's life. We were looking for "*the* song" that would leave a mark in music history. We were looking for a special "three minutes of music," a vehicle to carry the powerful message of the gospel of Jesus Christ.

It is the marriage of music and message that makes these songs so special. In this book, Lindsay Terry has captured the essence of many of the songs we love. Each story in this book represents inspiration, talent, effort, and diligence on the part of the writers who have penned the lyrics and the music. Lindsay's telling of the stories behind the time and effort spent in the songwriting process will enlighten and inspire the reader.

When asked to write this introduction, I was honored to try to encourage each reader to spend time thinking about the circumstances behind the great songs that are in this book. My heartfelt thanks to Lindsay Terry for writing the stories of the beginning of our songs; stories that would not be told without his help.

—GARY McSPADDEN

A Brief History of Southern Gospel Music

*W*hen we think of Southern Gospel Music, many names immediately come to mind—Mosie Lister, Les Beasley, George Younce, Bill and Gloria Gaither, Jake Hess, Naomi Sego Reader, Dottie Rambo, Calvin Wills, and Howard and Vestal Goodman. These are only a few of the many well-known personalities of this genre of Christian music. They, along with hundreds of others, carry on a tradition that had its beginning in the mid-1800s.

During those years, Ephraim Ruebush and Aldine Kieffer were most active in the spread of Southern Gospel Music, as it came to be called. Ruebush and Kieffer were the originators of a scale that allowed for a more complete harmony in the arranging of songs. Until that time, many Southern songs were sung using a scale of four notes, which came to be known as Sacred Harp. Kieffer and Ruebush used seven shaped notes to denote each pitch on the scale. Students of gospel music were taught in "singing schools" to use that method, and some music is still published today in shaped-note form.

James D. Vaughn was another major player in the development of Southern Gospel Music. Credited with having started the traveling quartet movement, he was also a publisher of songbooks. Some call Vaughn the father of Southern Gospel Music, while others use the term *founder*.

During the years that followed Ruebush and Kieffer's

development of the shaped-note scale, singing schools became very popular, especially in rural communities. They were often held in churches or other common meeting places, and people who wanted to learn the shaped-note system of singing flocked to those schools. Albert Brumley taught more than fifty of these singing schools before devoting himself full-time to the writing of songs. His first published song was "I'll Fly Away" in 1931. In the early to mid-1900s, Brumley was the most prolific Southern Gospel songwriter in America. Traveling quartets and radio programs carried his musical messages across our nation, and researchers for the Smithsonian Institution called him "the greatest white gospel songwriter before World War II."[1]

E. M. Bartlett Sr., who died in 1941, was the founder of the Hartford Music Company and the Hartford Musical Institute, which launched the careers of many successful writers and teachers. Bartlett wrote hundreds of songs, including "Victory in Jesus."

I would be remiss not to mention some other important pioneers of Southern Gospel Music: V. O. Stamps, Frank Stamps, James Blackwood, Lee Roy Abernathy, G. T. "Dad" Speer, Hovie Lister, J. D. Sumner, and Bob Wills. Others, just as talented and influential, could be added to the list.

Since shortly after the turn of the twentieth century, Southern Gospel Music has seen unusual acceptance and appreciation. But in the past two or three decades, the growth and popularity of the songs and the traveling groups who sing them have been phenomenal. From the first traveling quartet, in the mid-1800s—made up of James D. Vaughn and three of his brothers—the number of singing groups in the United States may now number as many as eight thousand. Today, thousands of dedicated young people are enthusiastically involved with Southern Gospel Music, indicating that the tide will continue to swell. Some of these are part-time groups that sing for special occasions and on weekends, whereas others keep a full schedule throughout the year.

The Gaither Homecoming videos and concerts have created a stir, causing interest in Southern Gospel Music to skyrocket. This renewed interest has helped many of the older Southern Gospel greats become even more recognized and popular. Some who had left the road have been called back out and are now appearing regularly in concert. A prime example is James Vaughn Hill, a former member of the Stamps Quartet and the Statesmen Quartet, and the composer of "What a Day That Will Be."

Part 1

Stories of Southern Gospel Songs

1

A Bassoon Player Turns Songwriter

He Came to Me

John 1:1–13

*He came unto his own, and his own received him
not. But as many as received him, to them gave he
power to become the sons of God, even to them that
believe on his name.*

As a child in the 1950s, Squire Parsons would sit with a reel-to-reel tape recorder and practice singing into it. He sang the lyrics of songs as well as the syllables of the shaped notes in the music, according to the method of singing developed by Ephraim Ruebush and Aldine Kieffer in the mid-1800s and passed on to thousands of would-be singers in popular "singing schools." Parsons was born into a musical family. His dad was the song leader of his home church, Newton Baptist Church in Newton, West Virginia, where Squire was saved at age nine.

During his high school and college years, he took all of the music training he could squeeze in. In college, he majored in music, with a proficiency in the bassoon. He had already learned to play the piano by ear, but his keyboard professors quickly changed that practice. He was trained and constrained to play by the notes on the page, a discipline that became an immeasurable blessing in later years.

After college, he began teaching at Hannah High School in

Mason County, West Virginia. He was hired as a band director, but his love for vocal music was so intense that he also started a school choir. At the height of the Vietnam War, he thought surely he would have to go into the armed services—he was classified 1A—but the principal of the school took advantage of the draft board's practice of allowing deferments for school-teachers, and thus Squire was able to stay on as an employee. It was a small, rural school, unattractive to many other teachers, but he quickly fell in love with the faculty and students. What was to be a temporary venture turned into four wonderful years.

It was while in Mason County that he wrote his very popular "Sweet Beulah Land." He has since written more than eight hundred songs, with approximately five hundred of them being published and recorded. Squire chose 280 of his songs and published them in a book titled *The Songs of Squire Parsons: The Millennial Collection.*

Squire had a second job during those years at Hannah High. He was a minister of music at various churches, two of which would not allow any gospel music at all. One of the churches, Christ United Methodist Church in Charleston, West Virginia, employed him as a bass soloist. Squire told me, "They were such gracious people. It was a wonderful experience." It was his first exposure to a more classical church music ministry. Squire continued, "I was there for two years, and during that time the people had a crushing blow: their beautiful sanctuary burned. The following Sunday, the pastor said, 'All of our music was in that building, and I know you love the gospel hymns. Is there one that you would like to share?' I chose 'Does Jesus Care?' That was the only nonclassical song that I ever sang there."

According to Squire, being in those churches influenced some of his writing in later years. It also helped when he went into churches that were not greatly influenced by Southern Gospel Music. He said, "I was not completely caught off guard when I went to those types of churches. I could identify with them, and I am thankful for that."

On weekends when he was not involved with the work at Hannah High or one of the churches, he sang with the Calvarymen Quartet, a group made up of Squire, his brother, and three other singers. After four years, he left the Calvarymen and Hannah High School and became a part of the Kingsmen, a Southern Gospel group of some note at that time.

Let me have Squire tell you how he wrote "He Came to Me":

"For years I had been under the impression that when I became a Christian, *I* found the Lord. As I became more and more involved with the Word of God and began to pay closer attention to sermons I heard preached, I found that God was coming to man. From the first part of Genesis through to the end of the Bible, there are so many instances where God moved upon men and called them to Himself. The idea of God's loving pursuit of man stayed on my heart for many years. As I looked at my own life, it became more and more evident that God had searched me out. He had come to me!

"One day as I was driving along, with my tape recorder on the seat beside me, I began to think about how God had come to me and saved me. I punched the record button on the machine and began to sing. The song was dropped into my heart, and it was a message that I wanted to share with other people.

"I am a member of Trinity Baptist Church in Asheville, North Carolina, and so I first sang it for my church family. Soon after that, I recorded it. In fact, it became the title song on my third album."

The gulf that separated me from Christ my Lord,
Was so vast, the crossing I could never ford.
From where I was to His demand, it seemed so far.
I cried, "Dear Lord, I cannot come to where You are."

Chorus:
He came to me. He came to me.
When I could not come to where He was, He came to me.

That's why He died on Calvary,
When I could not come to where He was, He came to me.

He came to me when I was bound in chains of sin,
He came to me when I possessed no hope within.
He picked me up and drew me gently to His side
Where today, in His sweet love I now abide.

Squire Parsons continues to crisscross America, singing and writing his songs as he shares his glorious testimony of the grace of God. He and his wife now make their home in Leicester, North Carolina, near Asheville.

Reflection

Mankind would be in a deplorable state had God not come down to earth and given Himself for our sins. He truly came to all of us. We must accept Him and let Him draw us into His family.

2

A Field of Cockleburs and a Two-Dollar Guitar

He Was There All the Time

Revelation 3:14–22

Behold, I stand at the door, and knock: if any man hear my voice, and open the door, I will come in to him, and will sup with him, and he with me.

In 1977, on a national television program, Bill and Gloria Gaither were asked, "How can you cowrite songs with a man like Gary S. Paxton?" Bill's answer: "Gloria and I are called to comfort the disturbed, and Gary is called to disturb the comforted."

As you will see in the following story, Gary S. Paxton has led a very unusual life from day one. In 1976, he recorded a gospel album titled *The Astonishing, Outrageous, Amazing, Incredible, Unbelievable, Different World of Gary S. Paxton*. The song "He Was There All the Time" was on the album, among eleven others with extraordinary titles such as "What'cha Gonna Do When You Ain't a Kid No More."

Gary S. Paxton was born in Coffeyville, Kansas, in 1939, to a very young, teenage mother who would later commit suicide. He was adopted by a Mr. and Mrs. Paxton and brought into a very humble home on a farm near Coffeyville. They afforded him no modern conveniences, such as running water and electricity, but loved him and taught him valuable lessons from the Bible.

When Gary was only ten years old, he bought his first musical instrument, a two-dollar guitar, with money he earned by hoeing thirty acres of land, freeing it of cockleburs, a coarse weed with thorns. It took him more than a month to complete the job. Sometime later, he moved up to an eleven-dollar Silverstone guitar that he found in a catalog.

Gary told me in our interview that he began to write songs at age ten, but those ventures were interrupted by a siege of spinal meningitis, which crippled him for more than two years. When he was fourteen, his family moved to Tucson, Arizona, where he started his own rockabilly band. Leaving his parents' biblical teachings and becoming engrossed with his musical activities, he dropped out of school after the eighth grade. He left home at age sixteen. A year later, he had written and recorded his first million seller, a song titled "It Was I." It was recorded under the name of Skip and Flip—in reality, Gary S. Paxton and Clyde Battin. This quickly led to a tour with Dick Clark and another million seller, "Cherry Pie."

The very next year, Gary had another million-selling record, "Alley Oop!" but by this time he had moved to Hollywood, where he became a part of the hippie movement with all of its drugs and alcohol. Over the next several years, he recorded or produced a number of million-selling records and worked closely with a myriad of stars such as Paul Revere and the Raiders, Leon Russell, The Association, the Four Freshmen, and others.

In 1969, at age thirty, he was the owner of several recording studios, a bookstore, a marina, a mountain hotel, a house rental business, and had his own radio show. But by 1970, the effects of the alcohol and drug abuse, plus the deception of business partners, had taken their toll and his "empire" crashed around him. He loaded as much as he could get into a U-Haul trailer and moved to Nashville, Tennessee, where he became a songwriter for a salary of one hundred dollars per week. He was jailed several times because of drugs and alcohol. By his own admission, he was a weird sight walking down music row with his long blond hair, a helmet with horsehair attached to the back, Hitler-style boots, and a Danish sword strapped to his side.

One day in 1971, he stumbled into Belmont Church, right on music row, where Amy Grant and Michael W. Smith attended at the time. He was grateful that the church members didn't throw him out because he was stoned. The following week, not loaded quite as much with drugs, he attended again. Because as a child he had been taught the Bible by his parents, and because he had begun to listen to the television messages of Dr. Robert Schuller and Dr. Charles Stanley, and because he had several musician friends who were Christians, he was ready for the clear, gospel-filled sermons of pastor Don Finto. He then gave his heart and life to Christ, and under the teachings of Pastor Finto he began to grow as a Christian.

In 1975, while reflecting on God's patience with mankind, and the fact that Christ will not force Himself on any of His creations, Gary wrote "He Was There All the Time." The song is something of his personal testimony. He had wandered far from the ways of the Lord and his parents' biblical teachings, yet God was long-suffering with him, and in His time, Gary would surrender completely to Him. In the song, he also declares that he now has the answer, and life is "starting to rhyme." Never again will he "look for a fake rainbow's end," but he'll be grateful that Christ was "right there all the time."

"He Was There All the Time," first recorded by Sammy Hall, has since been covered by hundreds of artists, including such notables as James Blackwood, Truth, the Bill Gaither Trio, Dave Boyer, Doug Oldham, and Connie Smith. Gary told me, "I have had about twenty gold and platinum singles and albums, and have won a Grammy Award, Dove Awards, many BMI and ASCAP awards and citation plaques, but the greatest 'award' is my name written in the Lamb's Book of Life. That's worth more than all of the others."

One of Gary's most memorable and exciting times to hear his song "He Was There All the Time," was in Charlotte, North Carolina, as Sammy Hall sang it at a large convention of eighteen to twenty thousand people. Gary was blessed to witness their reaction to the song that God had so graciously given him.

In 1999, he moved to Branson, Missouri, where he met and married Vicki Sue Roberts. Miss Vicki Sue, as she is affectionately called, says that "He Was There All the Time" had an impact on her life and is now her theme song. Because of the song, she met Gary. They now work together to further the cause of Christ through music and the spoken word.

Gary only occasionally sings publicly anymore. Several years ago, he was hospitalized with a stomach disorder and was given several blood transfusions, through which he contracted hepatitis C—a devastating blow. That, plus the effects of an attack on his life in 1980 by a hired gunman, which left him broken and bleeding and not able to think clearly for six years, have caused him not to trust his memory. And so, on the rare occasions when this sixty-four-year-old singer/songwriter is persuaded to sing for a group, he does so with the use of a music stand and a set of lyrics printed quite large.

Gary S. Paxton continues to write Christian songs and to mentor young, aspiring musicians. He says, "My plans are three-fold—to keep writing music, to keep praying that someone will have the courage to cut one of my Truth songs, and to work on my health problems that were caused by being stupid and sinful when I was young and unwilling to listen. Unfortunately, most of us spend the first half of our lives trying to kill ourselves and the last half trying to stay alive. All in all, I want to be remembered for the blessings I have helped bring to the lives of people through the Christian music God has so graciously given through me."

Reflection

Today, take time to celebrate the One who loves us, gave Himself for us, and who was waiting patiently, "all the time," to free us from sin and give us abundant life.

3

A High, Holy Moment with Mom

Born Again

John 3:1–17

*Jesus answered and said unto him, Verily, verily, I
say unto thee, Except a man be born again, he
cannot see the kingdom of God.*

*M*any of the songs that are sung in American churches were
written by people in other countries, particularly England. But
very few songs considered to be in the Southern Gospel genre
were written by composers from other countries. The subject
of this story is a song written by an Englishman but composed
while he was visiting the United States. Southern Gospel singers, as well as those of a more traditional bent, have used it
with great enthusiasm.

Andrew Culverwell was born in Somerset, England, in the
small town of Chard. Before his teen years, he developed a
keen interest in music, which started with piano lessons. After
Andrew had been trekking weekly to the piano studio for two
years, a note was sent home to his parents, William and Rosa
Culverwell, that read, "Please don't continue to send your son
to piano lessons. He plays by ear, and it is a waste of our time
and your money." As a result, he never learned to read music.
His masterful ability on the keyboard is simply and completely
a gift from God.

By age twelve, he was writing sing-along choruses for the congregation of the South Chard Christian Fellowship, a practice that continued into his teen years. After writing eighteen choruses, he moved on to writing complete gospel songs.

In 1968, he accompanied an English evangelist, Rev. Harry Greenwood, to the United States as soloist and musician. Although the Greenwood Crusades were held in many countries of the world, one of their most memorable meetings, at least for young Andrew Culverwell, was in Florida. One evening after Andrew sang, a gentleman in the service, Mr. Don Clause, of Lakeview, Oregon, stood and declared, "I am going to fly this young man to California to record some songs." Shortly thereafter, Andrew was flown to Hollywood and taken to the Capitol Records studios where he recorded five songs—just after the Beatles had finished with their recording sessions. In only a few short years, Andrew Culverwell and his recordings had become known and appreciated to the point that he was asked to be a guest soloist on the national television program the *700 Club*.

When I asked Andrew to tell me how he came to write "Born Again," he said, "In the fall of 1973, my wife and I had gone to Columbus, Georgia, to visit some very good friends, Jimmy and Joy Shierling. It was a Saturday, and in the afternoon, Joy and my wife decided to go out to do a bit of shopping. I was left there alone by the beautiful lake. In their home they have a lovely, antique Chickering grand piano.

"I began to think of how we gain our salvation, and of the Gospel of John, chapter three, where we find the story of Jesus' meeting with Nicodemus. Jesus told him, 'Ye must be born again.' It all began to take shape in my mind and in about an hour and a half the song was completed. When the shoppers returned, I played and sang the song for them and they were very positive and enthusiastic about it. They assured me that it was some of my best work and predicted that it would be one of my most widely known songs. And they were surely right about that."

Andrew recorded the song a short time later, putting it on his next album, which he titled *Born Again*. His recording helped to make the song known to a degree, but it received a gigantic boost in 1977 when it was recorded by a young lady named Evie Tournquist, an artist with Word Records. The song has a happy, rhythmic pattern that lends itself to the Southern Gospel genre. It has been recorded hundreds of times and now appears in printed song collections.

When I asked Andrew if there was a time when he had heard his song performed that was unusually meaningful to him, he told me the following story:

"In 1995, I was visiting my mother in England. I remember that it was only four days before she passed away. It was on a Sunday evening and I was sitting with her, holding her hand. The television right by her bedside was on and suddenly, to my surprise, one of the Billy Graham special programs came on. And to my greater surprise and excitement, the choir began to sing 'Born Again.' I said to my mother, 'Mom, they are playing my song!' It was an electric moment that I shared with her, and I will never forget it. They don't have an abundance of religious programming on English television, and to have that special program on, on that particular Sunday evening was incredible! I thought, 'I went to America and wrote that song, and now I am back in England, and they are singing it at the Billy Graham Crusade.' That was the last thing my mother was able to enjoy. She had very little sense of consciousness after that evening."

In Culverwell's song, he expresses his testimony of his salvation experience: "Born again! There's really been a change in me." It is also a message of salvation to others as he reminds us of Jesus' declaration to Nicodemus, "Ye must be born again."

Andrew Culverwell became a citizen of the United States in 1976, the bicentennial year, and now makes his home in Pompano Beach, Florida, where he and his wife, Anne, are members of the Pompano Christian Fellowship. He also continues to minister to churches and other groups, mostly in the United States and England, and to date has written approximately 180 complete songs and choruses, of which ninety or so have been recorded.

Reflection

Just as Nicodemus, two thousand years ago, came face-to-face with the fact that he would have to be born again in order to be saved and go to heaven, you and I are also faced with the same blessed opportunity and plan of redemption.

4

A Part of a Thin Red Line

Beyond Understanding

Philippians 4:4–9

*And the peace of God, which passeth all under-
standing, shall keep your hearts and minds through
Christ Jesus.*

$\mathcal{A}$ few years ago in *Singing News* magazine, the leading publi-
cation for Southern Gospel Music, in an article by Roy Pauley,
a lineup of the Top Ten Southern Gospel Music songwriters
was presented. Along with such greats as Mosie Lister, Albert
Brumley, and Stuart Hamblen, they named Elmo Mercer. For a
little more than half a century, he has influenced this genre of
Christian music. His songs are found on record albums, cassette tapes, CDs, and videos, and in hymnals and choral arrangements. Elmo's "What a Grand Reunion Day" was part of
the Hollywood film *A Thin Red Line*—a war movie produced by
Twentieth Century Fox in 1998.

W. Elmo Mercer was born in 1932, near the small, rural town
of Pollock, Louisiana. When he was seven or eight years old, he
began playing tunes on the piano that his sister was learning
for her music lessons. He then began exploring on the keyboard, picking out tunes of the day, which gave rise to his own
piano lessons for the next two years. He later would make tremendous progress, thanks to Billy Byrd, a musician with the

famed country artist Ernest Tubb, who taught him chord structure and progressions.

At age thirteen, he wrote his first song, "Lonesome in the Saddle." From that secular beginning, he turned to gospel songs and a year later wrote "A Glimpse of Jesus," published by John T. Benson Publishing Company. To date, he has written more than sixteen hundred songs, and approximately six hundred of them have either been recorded or published. For ten years, Elmo was a staff writer at Benson, and for the next twenty years he was chief music editor. He retired from Benson in 1981.

Elmo has compiled more than two hundred gospel songbooks, including several in the popular "New Songs of Inspiration" series, which must be some sort of record and will probably never be matched. His *Crusade Choir,* volume 1, sold more than half a million copies. His piano and organ duet books have enjoyed great popularity, and his original compositions appear in numerous denominational hymnbooks. His songs have crossed traditional lines and are enjoyed by music lovers of more than one genre of Christian music. I was honored that he was the editor for *Sing of Him,* a choral book that I compiled and arranged in 1970. "Each Step I Take," another one of Elmo Mercer's very popular songs, has been recorded by hundreds of artists in many languages.

The music of Elmo Mercer is loved in Indonesia, Africa, South America, and in many European countries. *Singing News* also called Mercer "one of the most dominating forces in gospel music today." He has received thirty awards for his outstanding work. The Zondervan Corporation called him "one of America's favorite songwriters." He can be seen among the honored guests on two Gaither Homecoming videos, *Sunday Meetin' Time* and *When All God's Singers Get Home.*

Elmo and his wife, Marcia, have appeared throughout the United States and Canada in their music concerts and programs. They are members of Park Avenue Baptist Church in Nashville,

Tennessee, where Elmo has been pianist for thirty-eight years. He now looks a bit like a Southern colonel with his silver hair, mustache, and beard.

In 1962, Elmo began thinking about God's love, as offered in the Bible, and how it is completely beyond our understanding. Yet God, in His compassion and infinite wisdom, looked down on you and me and sent His only Son to die for us. In the song, Elmo expresses that he searched, even on his knees, for the answer to the question, "How could He love me that way?" Although we can't understand, merit, or explain God's love, we have the assurance that we will one day see Him, the Source of that love.

Reflection

Though we cannot understand or explain why God loves lost people, it is one of the great truths that we must accept by faith. And then we return God's love as best we can.

5

A Pastor and His Stand-Up Bass

Written in Red

Romans 5:1–11

*But God commendeth his love toward us, in that,
while we were yet sinners, Christ died for us.*

$\mathcal{G}$ordon Jensen's songs are widely appreciated and singers love to use them—first of all because they accurately present scriptural messages, and secondly because they are uniquely written. Wherever Gordon goes in his itinerant ministry, he is welcomed with open arms. Jerry K. Rose, past president of the National Religious Broadcasters, said, "There are certain names that are synonymous with gospel music. Gordon Jensen is one of those names. When he writes and when he sings, he makes a solid gospel statement that I enjoy listening to." Jensen's many awards and honors have not turned his head from his goal—to reach as many souls as possible with his biblical messages.

In a 2001 interview, Gordon told me the story behind his famous song "Written in Red":

"'Written in Red' has a similar message to some of my other songs about the Cross and the love of Christ. The seeds of this song came from another song that was written many years before.

"My family moved to Mesa, Arizona, when I was only eight years of age. We started attending a small church where the pastor would occasionally sing solos. I remember that he played a stand-up bass as he sang. I never really understood why. Apparently he was not comfortable without his instrument.

"One of the songs that he sang more often than others was 'A Crown of Thorns,' written by Ira Stanphill. In the chorus was the phrase, 'He wrote His love in crimson red.'

"As a young child, the line, 'He wrote His love in crimson red,' captured my imagination—the idea of a hand writing the word love in red. It was an image that stayed with me. Thirty-two years later, in 1991, it all came together in 'Written in Red.' I don't remember where I was at the time I wrote it. It was, perhaps, on a plane or in a hotel room. I don't need to have an instrument with me when I write a song, although I may go to an instrument to finish it out.

"It was recorded by a number of singers before it really caught on and became widely known. Henry and Hazel Slaughter were the first to cut it, followed by Rusty Goodman and Steve Brock. Lari Goss, who for a number of years sang with his brothers James and Roni as the Goss Brothers, and who now orchestrates and produces many albums, has been responsible for the song being on several CDs. When he had the opportunity, he would *pitch* 'Written in Red' to singers needing another song for their projects.

"Then one day Janet Paschal recorded it, and it really took off on its way to the Top Ten on the Inspirational Charts. Camp Kirkland and Tom Fettke have put it in choral form and choirs across America have sung it, helping it to be even more widely received.

"God has a way of coming back to us with what He does through us. In December of 2000, it was late at night in our home and my family was in bed. I had a few struggles and was going over some things in my mind. I sat down on the couch and turned on the television. Lo and behold, Janet Paschal was singing 'Written in Red.' It was from a video taped in the Holy Land, the place where Christ went to the cross for us. It really inspired me. I thought, 'God obviously gave me that song for the body of Christ.' It was being sung on the Trinity Broadcasting Network, which reaches many nations of the earth. My song was being heard around the world, and I thanked Him for it. I said to myself, 'Well, it's worth it.'"

In Gordon's song he vividly describes how God wrote His love on a hillside more than two thousand years ago. He reminds us that it was for you and me that Jesus died—the greatest love story ever told. At Calvary, Jesus said, "I love you," and it was written in letters of crimson.

From his home in Nashville, Gordon Jensen continues to travel the length and breadth of our nation, reminding all who will listen of the love of our heavenly Father—and all the time writing more songs for Christians to sing.

Reflection

When Jesus was crucified, He voluntarily took the guilt of your sins and mine to the cross with Him. As death drew near, the Son of God summoned all of His human strength and said, "It is finished." Can our finite minds even begin to fathom the depths of His love?

6

A Scribe from the Back of the Bus

I Am Redeemed

Titus 2:1–15

*Looking for that blessed hope, and the glorious
appearing of the great God and our Saviour Jesus
Christ; who gave himself for us, that he might
redeem us from all iniquity.*

*P*hil Cross grew up singing with his family group, the Gospel Sounds. He said, "I don't remember learning to speak any sooner than I was singing. The earliest memories I have are involved with gospel music."

Phil was born December 16, 1957, to Lawrence and Myrt Cross in Ringgold, Georgia. At age eleven, during a visit to his grandmother's home, he gave his heart and life to Christ. After he expressed his interest in becoming a Christian, his grandmother called for the preacher. Phil says, "While she was in the other room making contact with the preacher, I was making contact with God." He then became a member of the High Point Baptist Church in Apison, Tennessee, near Chattanooga.

His early music interest included drums, guitar, and voice lessons from Sieglinde Cierpke Brown, a voice instructor at Tennessee Temple University in Chattanooga. Soon thereafter he began his songwriting career and to date has written or cowritten more than 350 compositions, most of which have been recorded or published. Phil was the founder of Poet Voices, a quartet that became one of the leading groups of the Southern Gospel genre. In 2002, Phil disbanded Poet Voices to spend his time in songwriting, choir revivals, solo concerts, Bible conferences, revivals, and songwriting seminars. Members of Poet Voices, apart from Phil, have since joined other Southern Gospel groups.

The story behind "I Am Redeemed" is an exciting account, especially as it is told by the author, Phil Cross.

"I saw a need for a song such as 'I Am Redeemed' approximately ten years before it was actually written. I wanted to write a song that would be a celebration of our redemption. I have always filed song ideas away to be used or considered at a later time; therefore, I have an abundance of concepts and impressions on hand so that I can constantly be building songs over time. During that ten-year period, I was never far from the 'redemption' thought. I had read everything I could get my hands on concerning our redemption. I listened to taped sermons on the subject and talked to preachers about the doctrine of redemption. I had been preparing for the song for years.

"One late afternoon as I was traveling with Poet Voices through the Great Smoky Mountains of North Carolina, near Bryson City, I was driving our bus into a beautiful sunset—the silhouette of the mountains against a magnificent, colorful sky. Suddenly I began to sing, 'I Am Redeemed!' Although I was driving, I began to try to write down the words that were coming. The melody and the lyrics were being given to me at the same time. I got the whole lyric, which began, 'I was a slave in a foreign land, so very far from the Father's righteous hand. He rescued me one glorious day, brought me out, paid a debt I could not pay.'

"It seemed as if the Lord was singing the song to me that afternoon. I was getting the song so rapidly it was difficult for me to jot it down. So, I intentionally turned a curve a little sharply to wake someone up. The men were asleep in the back portion of the bus. One of the Poet Voices came forward, asking,

'What is going on?' I said, 'Get a pad and pencil and write these words down.' He wrote it just as I dictated it to him.

"The verses and the chorus were nearly an instantaneous inspiration. However, I later saw the need for a narrative to go with the song. It is the only song I have written where a narration is used. I wrote it as a result of spending time in the Word of God, study, and prayer. The attention to the subject of our redemption during the previous ten years was also very helpful in writing the narrative."

Soon after the song was written, Poet Voices recorded it, with Phil doing the narration. It immediately began to catch on. Phil said, "On a weekly basis people tell me that they have used 'I Am Redeemed' in their own ministry." The song went to number one on the *Singing News* charts and was named Song of the Year in 1998.

Some of the other songs written by Phil Cross that have gone to the number one spot on the charts are "Saved to the Uttermost," "When I Get Carried Away," "The Key," "Yes, I Am," and "Jesus Built a Bridge." Phil has been honored as songwriter of the year on several occasions by the *Singing News* Fan Awards, *The Voice* magazine, and the Southern Gospel Music Association. He was honored with a Dove Award for "Champion of Love" in 1987.

Phil lives in Ringgold, Georgia, a suburb of Chattanooga, Tennessee, with his wife, Rebekah, and their son, Gavin. They are members of the Morris Hill Baptist Church in Chattanooga, and Phil continues in all of the wonderful activities mentioned above.

Reflection

One of the most precious words in the Bible is *redeemed*. The meaning is steeped in the most loving act ever carried out on the face of the earth, the death of Christ our Savior on the cross. God, in the flesh, gave Himself that we might be redeemed!

7

A Tornado Heading Our Way

Peace in the Midst of the Storm

John 14:21–27

*Peace I leave with you, my peace I give unto you:
not as the world giveth, give I unto you. Let not
your heart be troubled, neither let it be afraid.*

*D*uring the last four decades, I have interviewed scores of songwriters and have received from them some pretty incredible stories behind their songs, but none has ever matched the story you are about to read. It was told to me by Stephen R. Adams, a native of Woonsocket, Rhode Island. He was born there in 1943 into the home of a Nazarene pastor.

He began to study music early in life—at age seven, to be exact. Bill and Gloria Gaither befriended and encouraged him as a teenager, and while he was still in his late teens, he played organ accompaniment for some of their concerts. He was also the organist at the church in Indiana where his dad had become pastor.

Stephen became a student at Indiana University and graduated with a degree in Aristotelian (Greek) philosophy, after which he earned a graduate degree in English literature. With his formal education completed, he married a young woman named Janet, began teaching school, and traveled part-time as an accompanist for Doug Oldham.

During a most interesting interview, Adams related an unusual story, which is still hard for me to visualize:

"In 1974, Jan and I lived in Urbana, Ohio, about forty miles from Xenia, a town of about twenty-five to thirty thousand people, where I was employed as church minister of music. We were in the midst of preparation for an Easter musical, and early one morning I left home, in bright sunshine, to drive to the church where I was to meet other men who had agreed to help build a special stage setting for the presentation.

"I reached the auditorium before the other men and suddenly heard the fire alarm sound. The church had a preschool Kiddy College, a group of about 220 children who were inside the building. I rushed to the vestibule of the auditorium where some painters, who were working at the church, were already helping the children down into the basement from the upper floors. I looked out the front door of the auditorium and saw three funnel clouds in the sky. A tornado was headed directly toward our church. I could see roofs of homes being ripped off and spun around in the sky as if they were toothpicks.

"I quickly went to every phone in the building, and they were all busy. I wanted to call my wife to make sure that she did not come in the direction of the church. I suddenly remembered a pay phone about a quarter of a mile down the street. I rushed to my car, a Delta 88 Oldsmobile, and sped toward the pay phone. The circular winds, which I later learned were clocked at 360 miles per hour, were just too much. I had to pull into a drive-under at the bank for protection. I soon became fearful that the building would collapse on me while I was still in my car. I looked toward Kennedy Corner Shopping Center, about three hundred feet away, and saw a man standing in the doorway of a Western Auto Store, motioning frantically for me to come in his direction.

"I drove quickly toward him, and when I reached the front of the store, the winds were so strong I couldn't get the car to come to a complete stop. I jumped out and ran inside. I then saw the man at the back of the store with his hands above his wife's head and heard him screaming, 'My God! My God!' I dived under a sofa nearby, and suddenly the whole Kennedy Corner Shopping Center came crashing down on us. I was instantly buried alive!

"I remember calling Jan's name and the names of my children, Craig and Chris, as the building crumbled. I prayed for them, thinking that I probably would never see them again. I then remembered the words of an old hymn I had heard while I was a student at Andover Academy in Andover, Massachusetts: 'Oh Jesus, I have promised to serve You to the end.' I then surrendered my future and my life to His control.

"I was in complete darkness under that sofa, and I wondered if I was dead. I then realized that I was indeed alive because I pinched my forehead and felt pain. I was unhurt, so I began to try to dig out. I screamed for help because I sensed that I was entombed. Nobody was answering, and so I felt some panic.

"After . . . I don't know how long, I was able to pull some debris toward me and soon saw a light. I then struggled through that opening to get myself free. As I looked around, I realized that our city lay totally in ruins. I went under the sofa with everything intact and came out a little while later and everything was gone.

"I saw a lady sorely wounded and I frantically tried to find my car in order to get her to some medical help. I couldn't find it. I saw a police officer, who I thought might help me locate my car, but he was in a trance. He couldn't speak. I then ran toward the church. During the half-mile sprint, I saw nothing recognizable. When I reached the church, I saw the pastor standing in the frame of a doorway. He informed me that the children had all been saved in the basement, but the church building was gone, along with his home next door. In the middle of the street lay a dead man who had been killed trying to save a little girl. I was reunited with my family at eleven o'clock that evening. They were all safe. I hugged them more closely than ever that night.

"Three days later, the pastor walked with me to the ruins of the shopping center, and we saw National Guardsmen digging through debris where my car had been. I began inquiring about my automobile, and one of them asked, 'Do you drive a Delta 88?' and I said, 'Yes.' He immediately turned to the other guardsmen and shouted, 'You can stop looking!' Someone had seen me get out of my car, but then they couldn't find me after the storm had passed.

"My pastor had lost everything except his family. We both stood there in tears. He said to me, 'You know, Stephen, the Lord doesn't promise that He will take us out of life's storms, but He does promise to be in the storms with us.' That was the kernel that I needed for a song. Several days later, I began to reflect on the events of that frightful day and my experiences with the Lord. Verses began to form in my mind. Soon I had finished the song, 'Peace in the Midst of the Storm.'"

In the song, Stephen reminds us that Christ is an Anchor and a Rock on whom we can cast our faith, and that Jesus rides with us in our "vessel," so we can have "peace in the midst of the storm."

Reflection

As we look through the Bible, certain words become greatly comforting and precious: *love, peace, forgiveness, happiness*–and the list could go on and on. But no word in the Bible is more precious in a time of trouble than *peace*.

8

Almost Thrown Away

Redemption Draweth Nigh

Luke 21:20–28

And when these things begin to come to pass, then look up, and lift up your heads; for your redemption draweth nigh.

"Gordon Jensen stands out as a writer and singer whom God has anointed to minister to the hearts of people everywhere," says Jim Cymbala, pastor of the Brooklyn Tabernacle in New York City. "His songs address themselves to the deepest part of the spiritual man, and his unflamboyant, but Christ-exalting delivery, make him a genuine blessing." Cliff Barrows, long-time music director for the Billy Graham Crusades, says of Gordon's songwriting, "A beautiful gift to use for [God's] glory."

Gordon Jensen was born in Windsor, Ontario, Canada, in 1951, the son of Frank and Marion Jensen. His appreciation for Christian music started early in his life. He said, "At age five, I heard a choir singing Norman Clayton's 'Now I Belong to Jesus,' and I was moved. A year or so later, while at home one day with my mother, I sensed my need for Christ and told her of my desire to be saved. She, then and there, led me to Christ. During those years, my family attended Bethel Pentecostal Church in Windsor.

"Although I had some early interest in music, it did not catch fire with me in a total way until I was eleven or twelve years old. I remember that we moved to Mesa, Arizona, when I was eight, and there my parents found a piano teacher for me. Although I did learn some things, I wasn't altogether excited about the experience. Three years later, my dad went to a concert in Phoenix to hear the Blackwood Brothers and the Statesmen Quartet, and he came home with an armload of records. When I heard those Southern Gospel songs, my imagination was captured—there was something bright and alive about it.

"I had three cousins in Mesa whose dad had taught them to sing in harmony, and they persuaded me to join them as a quartet. I was a very high bass singer. We didn't have a pianist, so I increased my interest in the keyboard and became our accompanist.

"When I was fifteen, our family moved to Detroit, Michigan, where we attended Brightmoor Tabernacle, a very large church with a tremendous music program. There I met Larry Orrell, who invited me to join his singing group, the Orrells. We had a measure of success, even recording four albums with Zondervan's Singcord label.

"Larry's dad was a successful promoter of Southern Gospel concerts, booking many of the popular touring groups, such as the Speer Family, the Blackwood Brothers, and the LeFevre Trio. They filled auditoriums up to five thousand in attendance. Larry's dad scheduled us to sing first on each program—to warm up the crowd. The audiences weren't overly thrilled about that, but Mr. Orrell was the promoter.

"At age seventeen, I became much more interested in songwriting and began those ventures in earnest. About that time, the Orrells signed a recording contract with the Benson Company on their Heartwarming label. I wrote all of the songs for our records. And because we were singing in concerts with more popular quartets, those groups naturally heard my songs, and some of them began to record them. I was then offered a contract with the Benson Company as a staff writer.

"During my eighteenth year, there was an extensive amount of emphasis placed on eschatology—the rapture of the church in particular. It was a subject that was very meaningful to me, and a thrilling prospect. During those days, while hearing a lot of sermons, discussions, and songs about the coming of Christ and the signs of His return, I wrote 'Redemption Draweth Nigh.' Because the writing process took a very short amount of time, I did not have a huge regard for the song. It was hard for me to show it to others.

"Shortly thereafter, while in a concert with the Orrells and a famous quartet, I pitched my song to that popular group. They at first turned it down with the explanation that 'nobody wants to hear about war and strife,' which was a part of the second verse. I experienced a sense of rejection and defeat. I almost threw the song away and could hardly bring myself to show it to anyone else.

"Shortly thereafter, I mustered up enough courage to allow 'Redemption Draweth Nigh' to be recorded by the Orrells. Duane Allen of the Oak Ridge Boys just happened to be in the studio during our session and heard two of my songs, 'Redemption Draweth Nigh' and 'The Coming of the Lord.' Immediately he said, 'I will publish both of those songs.' He then added, '"The Coming of the Lord" will be a big hit, very quickly, but then it will die out. "Redemption Draweth Nigh" will start slowly, in my opinion, and will be around for a long time.' His predictions were very accurate. People eventually began to record 'Redemption Draweth Nigh' and today hundreds have done so—and it still continues. The famed quartet that turned it down in the beginning later recorded it.

"The Downings, the Sammy Hall Singers, and the Galileans were greatly responsible for getting the song out to the masses of the Southern Gospel fans, and Doug Oldham carried it to another genre of Christian music. Ron Huff's choral arrangement lifted it into yet another realm. It is wonderful to hear my song done by a large choir and orchestra."

Gordon's song speaks to all of us as he reminds us in a very explicit, biblical fashion that we are not to lose hope but instead lift up our heads and keep our eyes toward the eastern sky, remembering that our redemption, the coming of Christ, draws nigh. It is a musical reminder of those truths spoken of in Luke 21.

Gordon, his wife, Marsha, and their four children, Kellie, Hollie, Gordon II, and Michael, live near Nashville. He averages approximately 150 personal appearances each year throughout the United States, Canada, the West Indies, and into Europe and Africa.

Reflection

Many of us can identify with Gordon Jensen, in that we too have heard for many years that Jesus will come again some day. By faith in God's Word, we keep the promise real in our lives. Continue looking for and expecting our Lord to return. It may be today!

9

Angels Visited My Piano Keys

What a Healing Jesus!

Psalm 147:1–20

He healeth the broken in heart, and bindeth up
their wounds.

Unfolding Majesty, hosted by Dean and Mary Brown and featuring outstanding singers from across America, is one of the most popular programs on the Trinity Broadcasting Network. The program is made up of music that lifts the hearts of Christians and sends a message of hope to the needy. Dean is the emcee while Mary plays beautiful accompaniment on the piano and often helps to guide the flow of the music. Roni Goss, a regular on the program, supports the whole musical cast on the electronic keyboard. The program is seen by millions around the world who tune in to the weekly telecasts.

Mary Brown was born in 1948, in Tyronza, Arkansas. Her parents, Melvin and Lillie Young, were farmers who loved their children very dearly and afforded them every opportunity to advance in their chosen vocations. Mary was saved at age six and now says, "I knew from the moment that I could imagine my future that God loved me and had a plan for my life. My parents instilled that into me. They were fervent about Christian education as well as other academics."

At the tender age of five, a year before her formal piano

lessons began, Mary played one of her own compositions during one of her sisters' recitals. She says, "I grew up on the piano bench." Her regular piano instructions continued through her college years. When her sisters went away to college, Mary became the pianist at her home church, even though she was only nine years old! Although she could play by ear, she studied diligently, practicing every day, even before going out to play after school.

Mary related, "One of my earliest memories is of going with my family on Saturday nights to the Ellis Auditorium in Memphis to hear such famed Southern Gospel groups as the Blackwood Brothers and the Statesmen Quartet. We lived only an hour away." By age eight, Mary was singing in a trio with her sister Carolyn Young and her cousin Joyce Strickland. Mary said, "We sang together until I went away to college. A real highlight for us came when we were chosen as winners in the first singing contest ever held during the annual National Quartet Convention."

As a young teen, while others were listening to rock music, Mary would pull out recordings of the Goss Brothers—James, Lari, and Roni—and listen to their unique harmonies. She said, "It was my ear training. They were so unique and good." Little did she realize that years later she and Dean would record four albums with the Goss Brothers.

Mary said of her songwriting: "I never dreamed that I could write songs. I thought I would get my degree in music and teach classical piano for the rest of my life." Shortly after graduating from the prestigious George Peabody College for Teachers in Nashville, with a bachelor's degree in music education, Mary and Dean were married. They shared many of the same dreams and aspirations, so three years later they acquired a motor home and went on the road full-time to share their musical messages.

"During the early part of our ministry, as Dean would drive, I would read the Scriptures out loud. We were spiritually hungry. One day I found myself singing verses right out of the Bible. I didn't plan to do it; it just happened. I then began to write the music down as I sang. We joyfully learned the Scripture songs together and concluded that this process was very beneficial to our spiritual growth. We agreed, 'If this sort of thing is helpful to us and makes us grow spiritually, then it will feed our listeners too.' That is how I began my songwriting."

The following is Mary's account of how she wrote her famous song, "What a Healing Jesus!": "The real message began in me when I was a child. I came to realize that Jesus heals us physically and spiritually, and that He supplies our every need. I had lived on a farm where we depended on the Lord for rain, for the rain to stop, for sunshine, for good crops, for healing during our sicknesses, for good weather to gather the crops— we looked to God for everything.

"One day in 1989, when Dean and I were at home in West Memphis, Arkansas, we had the television on and were not particularly listening, but we could hear what was being said. I was busy about the house and as I walked through the room I heard a preacher say, 'What a healing Jesus You are.' It was not a profound statement, but it registered with my spirit that day. I asked, 'Dean, did you hear what he just said?' He answered, 'Yes, that is a nice phrase.' I immediately went to the piano and began singing the chorus to what is now 'What a Healing Jesus!' I feel that the heavens opened up and the angels came down to my piano keys. I then wrote two verses to go with the chorus I had written."

Dean and Mary recorded the song and began to sing it from place to place. Mary added, "James Blackwood, Walt Mills, Edith Tripp, and a number of others picked it up and began to sing it. It appears on one of the Gaither Homecoming videos. Paul Ferrin put it in choral form for choirs to sing. There have been times when it could be heard several times a week on television. It has been translated into Chinese and put into a beautiful Taiwanese hymnal. Letters have been received from a great

portion of the world, with people telling me that they are singing the song. I don't know how many languages that would
include."

Dean and Mary reside in Cordova, Tennessee, a suburb of
Memphis. They are members of the First Assembly of God
Church in Memphis. Mary Brown continues to write and thus
far has completed 125 compositions, many of which are her
Scripture songs.

Reflection

We, as Christians, have living within us the wonderful Healer
whom Mary tells about in her song. He wants His followers to
depend on Him for their every need, in every circumstance
and aspect of their lives.

10

Astounding Questions for Mary

Mary, Did You Know?

Luke 2:12–20

*Mary kept all these things, and pondered them in
her heart. And the shepherds returned, glorifying
and praising God for all the things that they had
heard and seen, as it was told unto them.*

*M*ark Lowry, a former singer and funny man of the Gaither
Vocal Band, was born in Houston, Texas, June 24, 1958. He
learned to love music as a young child, often singing as his
mother, Bev, played the piano. During his teen years he developed a love for Southern Gospel Music, especially the songs of
the Singing Rambos.

Although he was offered a scholarship to a college in Jacksonville, Florida, he decided to attend Liberty University in
Lynchburg, Virginia, where his older brother had studied. One
might think he would have been a member of a number of college singing groups, but he was never given the opportunity—
with one exception. He was asked to sing in a group formed by
Dr. Sumner Wemp, called the Preacher Boys Chorale. He said of
the experience, "I was the only one in the group that was not a
preacher, and the only one in the group that could sing."

After becoming a member of the Gaither Vocal Band, he
grew to be one of the most recognized and popular individuals

in Southern Gospel Music. In 2000, he carried his Christian comedy and his music to the Beacon Theater on Broadway in a show called *Mark Lowry on Broadway*. The Gaither Vocal Band joined him in that endeavor. For a time, a videotape of the performance was one of the fastest selling videos, of any kind, in America.

Although Mark is not known as a songwriter, "Mary, Did You Know?" caught the attention of Gospel Music fans. Here's the story behind the famous song, just as Mark told it to me:

"In 1984, I was living in Houston when Dr. Jerry Falwell called and asked me to write the program for the next Living Christmas Tree. I had never done anything like that before, but anything he would ask me to do I would try, if for no other reason than to see if I could do it.

"I took Christmas songs and wrote monologues to go between them. That was all I knew how to do. The songs were the standards that we know. As I wrote the monologues, I began to think about Mary. I have always been fascinated with the concept that God came to earth.

"In a conversation with my mother, I remember she said, 'If anyone on earth knew for sure that Jesus was virgin born—Mary knew!' That was a profound statement to me, and it stuck with me. I often thought of it. That was one thing they couldn't take from Mary. No matter what she was to endure, that *one* thing she could hold in her heart. She always knew. She knew that Jesus was no ordinary child.

"At the cross, while Jesus was dying, Mary's silence was a great testimony to the reality of who Christ is. He was dying for claiming to be God, not for healing the sick. He was dying because He 'blasphemed' to the Pharisees and the Sadducees. He said to them, 'When you have seen Me you have seen the Father.' Of course, they nailed Him to a cross, and His mother never said a word. A Jewish mother whose son is dying for claiming to be God would be saying something, but Mary said nothing.

"As my mind went back to the manger scene, I began to think about the power, authority, and majesty she had cradled in her arms. Those little hands were the same hands that had scooped out the oceans. Those little feet were the same feet that had been worshiped by angels. Those were the same lips that had spoken worlds into existence. All of that was contained in the little form that was now cradled on her bosom. Even now, He was the very same one who had given life to His mother.

"The beauty of Christ was that He became 100 percent man. He was just as much man as if He had not been God, and just as much God as if He had not been man.

"I began writing a list of questions that I would ask Mary if I could sit down with her. Not only questions about Jesus' life as a little boy and as a teenager but questions such as: Mary, do you know what is in your arms? Do you have any idea? All of heaven, all that holds creation together, and everything that holds you together is lying helpless in your arms. That is amazing!"

A very popular song grew out of the list of questions that Mark Lowry would have liked to ask Mary—questions such as, "Did you know that your Baby Boy would one day walk on water?" or give sight to a blind man, or calm a storm with His hand? The answers to those questions is wrapped up in the fact that He was and is the great I Am!

Mark carried the lyrics with him for the next seven years. He had asked a number of musicians to write a proper musical setting for it but had not yet found one that satisfied him. In 1991, he asked his good friend Buddy Green to write the music, and Buddy composed the beautiful melody that became the recorded song. After writing it over a weekend, Buddy called Mark on Monday and sang it to him over the phone. Mark's simple reply was, "That's it."

In a few short years, "Mary, Did You Know?" has become an extremely popular song, especially at Christmastime. It was first recorded by Michael English, and then by Kathy Mateo. Kenny Rogers and Wynonna Judd sang it as a duet. Donnie Osmond and the opera singer Kathleen Battle are two other prominent performers who have recorded the song. It was also performed during a Boston Pops Orchestra Christmas special, and Bruce Greer wrote a Dove Award-winning Christmas musical based on the song.

"Mary, Did You Know?" continues to grow in popularity and has been sung by countless Southern Gospel groups, choirs, special ensembles, and soloists across the United States.

Reflection

Since we're on the topic of asking questions, here's a question you should answer for yourself today. Do you know the Baby Boy, who is Christ the Lord, as your personal Savior? If so, do you nurture and cherish that relationship every day?

11

At the End of My Rope

One Day at a Time

Deuteronomy 33:24–29

As thy days, so shall thy strength be.

*M*any of the songs that are meaningful to Christians were born out of human adversity. That would be an understatement concerning the writing of the song "One Day at a Time." Its author, Marijohn Wilkin, went from one mountaintop of joy and success to another, but between those peaks were valleys filled with excruciating mental suffering.

Ernest and Karla Melson were blessed with just one child, Marijohn, born to them in Kemp, Texas, in 1920. Ernest played violin, piano, or led the singing at First Baptist Church of Sanger, Texas, and Marijohn quickly followed in her father's musical footsteps. By age five, she could play the piano by ear, and one year later, when her hands had grown a little larger, she could immediately repeat the songs she heard her father play.

A straight-A student, by age fourteen Marijohn was thrust into the family business, Melson's Veribest Bread, when Ernest was stricken with cancer. She did a variety of tasks, from store deliveries to working in the plant. Before his death three years later, which was a devastating blow to Marijohn, Ernest secured a twofold promise from her that she would go on to college to study music, and that she would take care of her mother.

Though she spent long hours in the bakery, Marijohn graduated as salutatorian of her high school class. This, coupled with her tremendous musical ability, earned her a scholarship offer from Baylor University. She attended Baylor for a short time before opting for a smaller school, Hardin-Simmons University, where she also was granted a full scholarship. At Hardin-Simmons, she was invited to join the University Cowboy Band as the only female member ever. She excelled in college as a musician and a singer, and was given numerous unusual opportunities to travel and perform with the Cowboy Band.

Three years after she graduated from college, Marijohn's husband, Bedford Russell, whom she had married two months after commencement, was killed during World War II in South Africa, where he was a pilot. Rising above the sorrow, Marijohn continued as a schoolteacher and sang as an alto soloist in her church choir. She also made an attempt to write songs but thought so little of her efforts that she didn't keep the manuscripts.

By age thirty-seven, she had moved to Nashville, Tennessee, where she became one of the leading songwriters in the country music industry and founded Buckhorn Music Publishers. By this time, she had remarried and had a young son named John Buck. She wrote more than four hundred country songs, and many of them rose to the top of the charts. She was associated with such stars as Mel Tillis, Johnny Cash, Patti Page, Charlie Pride, Patsy Cline, Glen Campbell, and many others. One of her writers at Buckhorn Music was Kris Kristofferson. She published more than seventy-five of his songs.

Amid the acclaim, money, and success she enjoyed as a country music songwriter, Marijohn stopped attending church and eventually became addicted to alcohol. On more than one occasion, she attempted suicide. But God, in His merciful grace, spared her life.

At age fifty-three, Marijohn wrote her most famous song, "One Day at a Time." Here's the story behind the song, just as she told it to me:

"I really could not understand why I was having so much success in the country music field. Although I had enjoyed quite a rush as a country writer, I had reached the end of my rope. I truly felt that I had been called to be a gospel writer, but I couldn't seem to get there. I was in the music scene up to my ears in Nashville. Wherever it was 'happening,' I was there, helping to make it happen. Yet I became frustrated! I'd *had* it!

"I stopped by a small church and asked a young minister if I could talk with him. I found out later that I was the first person he had counseled. I drove up in my new, midnight blue Cadillac, dressed in a full-length mink coat with sparkling jewelry and my cowboy boots. I said, 'I have all kinds of problems.' He looked at me and said, 'You look like you don't have any financial problems.' I answered, 'No, I don't.' He said, 'You look pretty healthy.' I said, 'Well, I guess I am.' He then asked, 'What is your main problem?' I said, 'I don't know.' He didn't seem to know what more to say to me.

"At that point in our conversation, he said a funny thing, but it was okay, because it worked. He asked, 'Did you ever think about thanking God for your problems?' (Ephesians 5:20). I left his office and drove back home.

"When I reached the house, I found it was empty, and I was glad. I sat down at the piano and began to play and sing—out loud—the entire chorus to 'One Day at a Time.' 'That's all I'm asking from You. Just give me the strength to do every day, what I have to do.' It just dropped into my heart. And when I had finished singing, my 'Nashville mind' said, 'That's a hit!' That was the first thing that popped into my head. I then recognized that the song was a prayer—and I got some relief.

"I wrote the chorus on the back of an envelope as fast as I could write. I then continued to sing, 'Do You remember when You walked among men? Well, Jesus, You know, if You're looking below, it's worse now than then.' I wasn't quite sure the Lord knew where I was. I'd never quit believing in Him, but I

65

was in Nashville and God was in heaven, and never the twain shall meet. I really didn't know if God actually knew where I was. I realize that some don't believe that, but that was where *I* was at the time.

"The following morning, my mind went back to the song. I had the second verse and the chorus, but somehow I couldn't get the song started properly. Kris Kristofferson and Rita Coolidge, who were married at the time, were in town. They had just had a huge hit, 'Why Me, Lord?' written by Kris. Their recording had won a Dove Award for them. I called Kris and asked him to help me with the first verse. He had written songs for my company, Buckhorn Music, and we'd had some pretty big hits as a publisher.

"When I showed him how I started the song, 'I'm just a mortal . . .' he looked at me and said, 'Why don't you say, "I'm only human, I'm just a man . . ." I said, 'That's good! That's what I need.' We finished the first verse in about twenty minutes. The lines just flew out from each of us."

The song, first recorded by Marilyn Sellers, rose to become the number one song in several categories. In this country, it was first a hit on the country charts and then it crossed over to the pop charts. It was the number one pop song in England, the number one country song in Ireland, and among the top ten in two other countries. Each recording has been by a different artist in that particular country. It has long since passed the six hundred mark in artist recordings and has crossed over into the Southern Gospel Music genre.

Marijohn Wilkin, as a singer, went on to record four fabulous albums for Word Music. "One Day at a Time" was on the first album, which she titled *I Have Returned.* It was Marijohn's way of letting America know that she had come back to the Lord. She is now a happy, alcohol-free Christian and has written approximately three hundred gospel songs. In 1975, she was once again honored, this time with a Dove Award. She shared the platform with other winners, including Brock Speer and James Blackwood, both of Southern Gospel Music fame. She continues to make her home in Nashville.

Reflection

Though each day of our lives can bring seemingly insurmountable challenges, always keep in mind that God has stated He will never leave us or forsake us. Be at peace in His presence today.

12

Courage and Strength for His Child

Because He Lives

John 14:16–31

Yet a little while, and the world seeth me no more;
but ye see me: because I live, ye shall live also.

$\mathcal{I}$ daresay there is not a Southern Gospel Music fan on the face of the earth who has not heard at least one song written by Bill and Gloria Gaither. Millions of Americans and people of other countries are coming to love Southern Gospel, and most of them can name more than one Gaither song. The Gaither Homecoming concerts and videos are the primary reason. One of the Gaithers' best-known songs is the subject of this story.

When Bill and Gloria were single and teaching in the same high school, they met and began to share ideas about songs. Gloria, an English major in college, would become in later years the predominant writer of the lyrics in their songs, whereas Bill's forte was the musical setting. Their joint efforts, which began during their years of teaching, blossomed into the most prolific husband and wife songwriting team of modern times.

Bill and Gloria wrote their first song together some forty years ago. Their songs, almost without exception, started with an *idea*. Usually, Bill would write a musical piece with an idea in mind, and then Gloria, using the same idea, would write the words. On some occasions, Gloria revealed in her book *Fully*

Alive the whole lyric would come to her, and then Bill would write the music, either alone or with a cowriter. They have now written some six hundred songs and produced sixty recordings and several musicals. And both have authored or coauthored several books.

One of the couple's most admirable characteristics is their desire to assist other songwriters and musicians, especially youngsters. In my more than forty years of interviewing songwriters, I have met young people on several occasions who recounted to me their experiences with Bill and Gloria Gaither. At least one teenager, who today is a famous songwriter and musician, just showed up unannounced at their home one afternoon in Alexandria. He was invited to stay for supper. During the course of the evening, he was greatly encouraged.

Of late, many older singers and songwriters who had all but gone into retirement are now back out on the road singing from church to church and from one Gaither Homecoming concert to the next—thanks to Bill and Gloria. The Gaithers have cowritten with scores of songwriters in their home, in their Indiana studio, and in other locations. It is a boost to any songwriter to have his or her name appear at the top of a musical selection as a cowriter with Bill and Gloria.

The Gaithers' lives have not always been smooth sailing, however. During the late 1960s, while expecting their third child, they went through a rather traumatic time. While Bill was recovering from a bout with mononucleosis, he and Gloria and other members in their church family were the objects of false accusations and belittlement. It was a special time of fear and torment for Gloria. With all the craziness surrounding her family, the thought of bringing another child into the world was taking its toll on her.

She remembers sitting in their living room in agony and fear on New Year's Eve. Across the nation, the educational system was being infiltrated with the "God is dead" idea, while drug abuse and racial tension were increasing. Then, suddenly and quite unexpectedly, she was filled with a sweet, calming peace. Like an attentive mother bending over her baby, it was as if her heavenly Father saw His Gloria and came to her rescue. Her panic gave way to a calmness and an assurance that only the Lord can give. She was assured that the future would be just fine, left in God's hands.

Both Bill and Gloria remembered that the power of the blessed Holy Spirit seemed to come to their aid. The power of Christ's resurrection was reaffirmed in their lives and in their thoughts. To Gloria, it was "life conquering death" as joy once again permeated the fearful circumstances of their lives.

All of this gave rise to one of the most famous Southern Gospel songs of our time, "Because He Lives." The first verse is a presentation of the gospel of Christ, reminding us of His death, burial, and resurrection. In the second verse we see the life of a new baby and sense the assurance that Christ alone can give. The little one can have a victorious life because Christ lives.

As we realize that God holds the future and makes life worth living for all who trust in Him, we can face tomorrow with all the uncertainty it brings.

Reflection

As we remember Christ's resurrection, we gain assurance and strength to overcome the frightening obstacles of life. It is also very meaningful and empowering to realize that Jesus lives, every single day, in our hearts.

13

From a Handheld Recorder to the Nation

Out of His Great Love

Psalm 40:1–17

*I waited patiently for the LORD; and he inclined
unto me, and heard my cry. He brought me up also
out of an horrible pit, out of the miry clay, and set
my feet upon a rock, and established my goings.*

Terry and Barbi Franklin are young teachers, singers, and
songwriters upon whom God has placed His hand. He is blessing thousands through their ministry. They have sung in all
fifty states and in thirty-four countries. For the past eighteen
years, in addition to their music ministry, they have taught lessons on family integrity and a renewed hunger for God and
His Word. Their theme is "Inspiring Love in the Home and
Revival in the Church." Some of the people Terry and Barbi
have worked with include Billy Graham, the Brooklyn Tabernacle, Gary Smalley, Focus on the Family, Adrian Rogers, and
Josh McDowell. Though their work is widely praised, they are
not focused on the acclaim. "Our deepest desire is to please
God, not people," Terry said. "We desire to know the mind of
God and to focus on our ministry for Him, not on entertain-
ment." Dr. Jack Hayford said of the Franklins, "The thing I'm
most grateful for is the genuineness of their lives in the Lord."
Terry was born in Miami, Florida, in 1957. His parents, Bob

and Sandra Franklin, brought him up in the midst of harmony singing. Bob sang in a barbershop quartet that performed in a number of venues, including the *Jackie Gleason Show*. When Terry was saved at age nine, his life took on new meaning. Around the same time, he became an avid fan of Southern Gospel Music and each week was eager to see who the guests would be on the *Gospel Singing Jubilee*. When Terry was thirteen, God called him into His service and gave him the assurance that he would be in full-time music ministry in the future. After high school, he went away to Moody Bible Institute in Chicago, where he met Barbi Murk. After they were married, Terry sang tenor for the Gaither Vocal Band for two years, following Jim Murray at that position. Afterward, Terry and Barbi joined the Gaither concerts, often opening for them when their schedules would allow it.

Barbi was born in Chicago into a famous musical family. Her parents, Jim and Donna Murk, along with their children, Beverly, Bill, Becky, Brenda, and Barbi, traveled the length and breadth of our nation and to many other countries. In addition to their wonderful singing as a family group, all of the children played instruments, mostly violin, viola, or cello. Barbi was saved at the tender age of five and afterward rededicated her life to Christ on many occasions.

After Terry and Barbi began their ministry to families, they also began to write songs. Most of their music has a message to Christians, reminding us of the greatness and goodness of God and our relationship to Him. Their first noted and recorded song was titled "No Wonder," cowritten with the prolific Niles Borop. Here is their account of how "Out of His Great Love" came into being:

Barbi: "I remember it was in 1994, and I was in our family room at our home in Antioch, Tennessee. I was in a sincere time of prayer, seeking the Lord, when God began to speak to me out of His Word. He reminded me that it was out of His great love that He lifted us up and has done so many wonderful things for us. While learning about His unconditional devotion to us, I was blessed very deeply and turned it into a proclamation. I got this little thing in my mind and the music started to flow.

"After the lyrics were written and I had a melody running through my head, I brought it to Terry and said, 'Listen to this,' and I played it for him. He said, 'That's okay, but you have a northern beat to it. It would be much better with a southern beat.' We sat at the piano and recorded it on a small, handheld tape recorder, giving it a lilt and a decided Southern Gospel sound. We also emphasized the 'He picked me up' phrase in the chorus. We thought it sounded better that way."

Terry: "We sent the tape recording, along with the music manuscript, to Michael Sykes, the producer for the Martins. He liked the song so the Martins put it on their first project for Springhill. It became their first number one song on the *Singing News* and *U.S. Gospel News* charts, and received a Dove Award as Song of the Year in 1996. The Martins' recording of our song sent it to a higher level than we had anticipated."

The song is a testimony for all Christians, explaining how we had gone astray and lost our way, then we called upon God's name. We were rescued and given a song to sing, and what a loving heavenly Father we enjoy. The chorus is a restating of Psalm 40:1–2, quoted at the beginning of this story.

Among the artists who have recorded "Out of His Great Love" or other songs by the Franklins are Gold City, the Brooklyn Tabernacle Choir, Gerald Wolfe, Sue Dodge, and Glen Campbell. Although Terry and Barbi's songs are, for the most part, in the Inspirational genre, "Out of His Great Love," "Calvary Came Through," and "God of All Gods" are in the Southern Gospel Music vein.

At home, Terry also works as a studio musician, recording audition tapes, at times singing all of the parts. Barbi oversees the work in their offices. They write a monthly article for *U.S. Gospel News* and presently lead a weekly Bible study and worship time at the Heart for the World Outreach Center, located on the east side of Nashville. On the weekends, they continue their itinerant ministry. Their teenage sons, Travis and Tyler, who are homeschooled, join them on the road in their seminars, concerts, and workshops.

Reflection

We cannot now fathom the awesome, eternal love of our Savior. We must be content to accept it by faith, allowing it to be our comfort and assurance in every trial or sorrow. We can also let His love be our joy in every conquest and triumph.

14

From God, for God and His People

Peace in the Valley

Ephesians 2:11–22

For he is our peace . . .

One of the most prized possessions I have as a song historian is a cassette containing a recording of my interview with Thomas Andrew Dorsey, which he granted to me in 1977. In it he told me a great many things about himself and his music. Time and space will not allow me to tell his whole story, but I am passing on to you some of the highlights of his very active life as a musician, choir director, and songwriter.

Thomas Dorsey was born in Villa Rica, Georgia, a small town about forty miles from Atlanta. While still in his early teens, his attention was drawn to show business by the music of the black performers in Atlanta. He soon began playing piano in the jazz clubs, under the name of Georgia Tom. At age seventeen, he moved to Gary, Indiana, to pursue his music career. Two years later, he moved on to Chicago, where he enrolled in the Chicago College of Composition and Arranging and began playing with local jazz groups. He soon formed his own band, which became the backup group for Ma Rainey, a well-known blues singer.

In 1928, in partnership with slide guitarist Hudson "Tampa Red" Whitaker, he wrote and recorded a song that hit the top of the blues charts and sold more than seven million copies, according to one report. Dorsey is credited with writing more than 450 rhythm and blues and jazz songs, and with establishing the Dorsey House of Music in 1932, the first independent company to publish black gospel music.

Nevertheless, his life was proof that the world does not satisfy a Christian. After he suffered a nervous breakdown, it took two years for him to recuperate. During that time, the Lord was speaking to him. In 1930, he lost his wife and newborn son. He later said, "I was doing all right by myself, but the voice of God whispered, 'You need to change a little.'" He eventually found that he could not be a part of the R&B and jazz world and do his work for the Lord properly.

He put together a choir at his church, Pilgrim Baptist Church, with Roberta Martin playing the piano. In 1933, he organized the National Convention of Gospel Choirs and Choruses, along with Sallie Martin, his good friend Theodore Frye, and several others. During our interview in 1977, he told me that he was still actively leading one of the choirs at the church. He was seventy-eight years old at the time.

His songs have been recorded by such diverse artists as Mahalia Jackson, Tennessee Ernie Ford, and Roy Rogers and Dale Evans. President Lyndon B. Johnson requested that "Take My Hand, Precious Lord" be sung at his funeral. It was also used at a rally led by Martin Luther King Jr. the night before his assassination.

In September 1981, Dorsey's native state honored him with election to the Georgia Music Hall of Fame. In 1982, he was the first African-American elected to the Gospel Music Association's Living Hall of Fame. In that same year, the Thomas A. Dorsey Archives were opened at Fisk University, where his collection joined those of W. C. Handy, George Gershwin, and the famed Jubilee Singers. In summing up his life as a Christian, Dorsey said that all of his work has been "from God, for God, and for His people." In 1983, George T. Nierenberg produced a documentary of the history of gospel music, *Say Amen, Somebody*, in which Thomas Dorsey made a personal appearance. Dorsey was also elected to the Nashville Songwriters International Hall of Fame.

In 1937, he wrote a song for Mahalia Jackson, "Peace in the Valley," which has become extremely popular. I will never forget hearing a young black man walking down a road on Andros Island, an out-of-the-way part of the Bahamas, singing "Peace in the Valley." In the song, Dorsey speaks of being "tired and so weary," a plight of many of God's people who "must go along." But there is coming a time when the "morning is bright and the Lamb is the Light." In that time and place, the "night is as fair as the day" and there is no more sadness, sorrow, or trouble—only peace.

After the passing of Dorsey's wife, Nettie, he later married again. I had the joy of speaking with Mrs. Kathryn Dorsey shortly before her husband's death on January 23, 1993, in Chicago. Thomas Dorsey wrote nearly one thousand gospel songs in his lifetime.

Reflection

There is no word more precious than *peace*, nor a more joyous state of being for a Christian, than to know God's peace. We long for it, and when it comes to us it is directly from our heavenly Father.

15

From the Flippant to the Sublime

We Are So Blessed

Ephesians 1:1–14

*Blessed be the God and Father of our Lord Jesus
Christ, who hath blessed us with all spiritual
blessings in heavenly places in Christ.*

*L*ike many of the songs that have become standards in the
Southern Gospel Music genre, the writing of "We Are So
Blessed" was a group effort. When two or three songwriters
collaborate on a song, they build on each other's ideas and can
evaluate the quality of each other's writing. This collaborative
process improves the project line by line. When every member
of the writing group is extremely talented, as in the case of
"We Are So Blessed," the results can be quite memorable.

Greg Nelson was born in Bismarck, North Dakota, in 1948
into the home of musical parents, Corliss and Irene Nelson—a
singer and a pianist. Greg's dad sang in the operas and operet-
tas that he and his wife produced. They encouraged the participation of their children in the music of the community as
well as in their church. Greg made a profession of his faith in
Christ as a young child, which he later confirmed as a result of
the preaching of the late Dr. Bill Bright, founder of Campus
Crusade for Christ.

Along with his brother, Corliss Jr., and his sister, Sigrit, a child prodigy who could play the classics at age five, Greg learned piano and theory from his mother. Greg said, "I basically grew up in an orchestra. I also played with my brother and sister as a trio—Sigrit played piano, Corliss played violin, and I played cello. By age twenty-one I was conductor of the Bismarck Civic Orchestra."

Greg's musical background greatly contributed to the quality of the songs that have come from his heart and his pen. Having written or cowritten hundreds of songs, a large number of which have been recorded or published, he will no doubt go down in history as one of the great composers of Christian music. Among the favorites Greg has written or cowritten are "People Need the Lord," "There Is a Savior," "Calvary's Love," and "Lamb of Glory."

Here is Greg's account of how he cowrote "We Are So Blessed" with Bill and Gloria Gaither:

"In 1982, Bill and Gloria Gaither and I were visiting in the home of Bob MacKenzie, a music executive and long-term producer for the Bill Gaither Trio. As might be expected, music was the topic of our conversation. Bill began to express his concern about the treatment of a particular song he had heard on television. It was a song that spoke of the blessings of the Lord in our lives. He thought the song was being sung too lightly and too flippantly.

"He then said, 'Why don't we write a song describing how Christians are *so* blessed.' I expressed a few ideas concerning the music, but nothing beyond that was actually done during our visit. I took the idea and went back to my home and shortly thereafter wrote a musical setting. I later came back with the music completed and showed it to Bill. He, in turn, shared the music and the idea with Gloria, who wrote the lyrics. It was later recorded by the Bill Gaither Trio and many other groups."

Millions of people have sung "We Are So Blessed," and it has found its way into the hearts and hymnals of Christians everywhere. It is the repeated phrase, "we are so blessed," that makes the song unique. A better song of thanksgiving cannot be found. In Gloria's lyrics, acknowledgment is made of the Lord's blessings—when we are empty He fills us to overflowing, and when we are hungry He feeds us. His goodness is more than we can understand, and we cannot find an adequate way to express our true gratitude to Him other than to say, "We love You!"

Reflection

As we try to enumerate the blessings of the Lord, we become overwhelmed with His kindness toward us. "He that spared not his own Son, but delivered him up for us all, how shall he not with him also freely give us all things?" (Romans 8:32).

16

"Georgia Tom" Makes His Mark

Take My Hand, Precious Lord

Psalm 37:1–8

*Delight thyself also in the LORD; and he shall give
thee the desires of thine heart. Commit thy way unto
the LORD; trust also in him; and he shall bring it
to pass.*

In 1899, little notice was taken of the birth of Thomas Andrew Dorsey. He was around the church most of his early life because his father was a devout Baptist preacher and his mother was an organist. She started young Thomas on the piano when he was seven years old.

He became a Christian at age sixteen but left the things of the church a few years later to become an entertainer. He got a job in a club in Atlanta, where he met many of the vaudeville entertainers of that day. He then decided to embark on a career as a blues musician and was for a number of years billed as "Georgia Tom." He soon tired of that kind of life and felt constrained of the Lord to return to his Christian activities. He then began to write gospel songs.

Dorsey carried his blues rhythm into his gospel music, which caused his songs to be rejected by many of the church leaders. He later said, "I got thrown out of some of the best churches in those days. I felt like going back to the jazz field of music." Yet, he continued to write songs and to train his choirs. He built such a following that it was not long before people began to flood into churches to hear his music.

By 1920, his travels had carried him to Chicago, where he joined Pilgrim Baptist Church. Because of his rededication to Christ, the Lord allowed him to become a leader in the field of gospel music. Dorsey wrote about three hundred songs and directed choirs for more than fifty years, most of that time at Pilgrim Baptist.

When I interviewed Thomas Dorsey in about 1977, he was still the director of the Gospel Choir, one of four choral groups at the church, even though he was seventy-eight years old. He was also president of the National Convention of Gospel Choirs and Choruses. He told me the following story, which had happened forty-five years earlier. (I still have the tape of the interview.)

"My wife, Nettie, was about to bear our first child. I was called to St. Louis to sing in a revival. I wondered if I should go, because of my wife's condition. She persuaded me that I should go ahead.

"I asked a friend to go with me. When we were a good way out of town, I remembered that I had left my music case at home. I knew that I must have my music, so I drove back to get it. At that point, my friend decided that he would not make the trip with me after all. So I, alone in my Model A, drove to St. Louis.

"During the first night of the meetings, a lad brought a telegram to me while I was still on the platform. It was horrible news. It was a message that my wife had died giving birth to our son.

"I rushed to a phone while the people were still singing and found that the message was true. Mr. Gus Evans drove me back to Chicago that night.

"When I arrived, I found that the wonderful baby boy was seemingly fine, and yet, that night he also died. I buried my wife and little son in the same casket.

"During the next few days, I became very despondent. I was filled with grief. I had thoughts of going back to the world's music on Chicago's South Side, and yet I knew that God had taken me out of all of that.

"A few days later, I went over to Madame Malone's College, a neighborhood music school, to visit with my good friend Professor Frye. We walked around the campus for a while and then went into one of the music rooms.

"I sat down at a piano and began to improvise on the keyboard. Suddenly I found myself playing a particular melody that I hadn't played before. As I played I began to say, 'Blessed Lord, blessed Lord, blessed Lord.' My friend walked over to me and said, 'Why don't you make that precious Lord?' I then began to sing, 'Precious Lord, take my hand, lead me on, help me stand.'

"When I finished the song, we began to use it before it was published. So many people wanted a copy of it that we put a rush act on the printer and got the song out. And it has been going ever since. I have gotten letters from people all over the world. I have traveled better than halfway around the world myself. It was a great tragedy, but we got the message to the world."

Thomas A. Dorsey learned a marvelous lesson that day. The Lord healed his spirit and gave him back his song. He learned, like many others since that time, that when we are in our deepest grief, when we are seemingly far from God, He is still close to us. During those times we need His restoring power.

"Take My Hand, Precious Lord" has been translated into more than thirty languages and is sung in many countries around the world.

Reflection

The Lord will never leave us comfortless, nor will He forsake us. When we despair in the darkness of life's afflictions, we need only to reach out and He will be there to answer every need and bring us into the warm glow of His light.

17

Honored by the Smithsonian

Sweet, Sweet Spirit

James 5:7–16

*The effectual fervent prayer of a righteous man
availeth much.*

*D*oris Akers, born in Brookfield, Missouri, on May 21, 1923,
was one of ten children. She learned to play the piano by ear at
age six and by age ten had composed her first song. By the
time she was twelve, she had organized a five-piece band that
played music of the 1930s. When she was only twenty-two years
of age, she moved to Los Angeles, where she encountered a
thriving gospel music community. She met several outstanding
musicians, such as Eugene Douglas Smallwood, who greatly
influenced the gospel music career of this young African-
American lady. A year later, Doris joined the Sallie Martin
Singers as pianist and singer. Two years later, with Dorothy
Vemell Simmons, she formed the Simmons–Akers Singers and
also launched a publishing firm called Akers Music House.

In 1958, in a Los Angeles church, she started a racially mixed
gospel group, the Sky Pilot Choir, which featured African-
American gospel music. People would drive for miles just to
hear their song arrangements. Many artists, including the Stamps–
Baxter Quartet, Bill Gaither, George Beverly Shea, and Mahalia
Jackson, have recorded Akers's songs. Countless other Southern

Gospel Music groups still record and sing her music. Millions of church members have sung her songs, which have long been published in many hymnals. She was a recording artist, music arranger, choir director, and songwriter and was awarded Gospel Music Composer of the Year for both 1960 and 1961.

In 1958, she and Mahalia Jackson cowrote "Lord, Don't Move the Mountain," which won a Manna Music Gold West Plaque in recognition of one million records sold. She was honored by the Smithsonian Institution, which labeled her songs and records "National Treasures." She was inducted into the Gospel Music Hall of Fame in 2001, along with such notables as the Rambos and Kurt Kaiser.

When I interviewed her in the late 1980s, she related to me that one Sunday morning in 1962, while directing the Sky Pilot Choir, she said to her singers, "You are not ready to go in." She didn't believe they had prayed enough! They were accustomed to spending time with her in prayer before the service, asking God to bless their songs. She said, "I feel that prayer is more important than great voices." They had already prayed, but this particular morning she asked them to pray again, and they did so with renewed fervor.

As they prayed, Doris began to wonder how she could stop this wonderful prayer meeting. She said, "I sent word to the pastor letting him know what was happening. He was waiting in the auditorium, wanting to start the service. Finally, I was compelled to say to the choir, 'We have to go. I hate to leave this room and I know you hate to leave, but you know we do have to go to the service. But there is such a sweet, sweet Spirit in this place.'"

Doris explained to me, "Songwriters always have their ears open to a song. The song started 'singing' to me. I wanted to write it down but couldn't. I thought the song would be gone after the service. Following the dismissal, I went home. The next morning, to my surprise, I heard the song again, so I went to the piano and began to put it all down." She had been given the now-famous "Sweet, Sweet Spirit."

In her song she recognized the "Spirit in this place," as the "Spirit of the Lord." She could see in the "sweet expressions" of the choir members that they also recognized the "presence of the Lord." In the chorus of the song, she calls us to the New Testament where the Spirit of God descended like a dove, lighting upon Jesus at His baptism (Matthew 3:16). She calls Him "sweet heavenly Dove," asking Him to stay right there with them, filling them with His love.

To the end of her earthly life, Doris Akers believed that God wants His children to pray. Her songs have circled the globe, aiding Christians of all nationalities in their worship of the heavenly Father. She passed away on July 26, 1995, in Minneapolis.

Reflection

Not very much worthwhile was ever accomplished apart from prayer. The greatest example for our prayer lives was Christ our Lord, who felt the need of fellowship with the heavenly Father and took advantage of the opportunity on many occasions that are recorded in Scripture.

18

I Wept When I Heard the Story

Then I Met the Master

John 9:1–25

*One thing I know, that, whereas I was blind,
now I see.*

In 1953, the songs of Mosie Lister began to influence the music of the churches of America, and eventually those of other nations. Mosie's songs always give testimony to the greatness of our Savior. Singers too numerous to count have recorded and sung Lister's musical offerings. The messages from Mosie's heart, given to him by Christ, have brought joy and satisfaction to millions of God's people. Many traveling quartets made Lister's songs their own as they sang them in concert halls, on television programs, and in crowded churches.

A native of Georgia, Mosie grew up with music. Early in life he learned to play the violin, guitar, and piano. Later, the study of music theory and harmony began to interest him greatly. This background stood him in good stead as he penned hundreds of classic songs, most of which can be classified as Southern Gospel.

Mosie became a Christian at age seventeen and shortly afterward became completely enthralled with the spirit and the message of Christian music. It was not long before he began to be invited to sing with gospel quartets. Three years after his conversion to Christ, he joined his first singing group, the Sunny South Quartet.

A hitch in the navy interrupted his music ministry, but soon after being discharged he resumed the career he loved—Christian music. It was not long until he was a member of one of the most famous singing groups in America, the Statesmen Quartet.

Those experiences were just the beginnings of an illustrious journey that caused him to be one of the most influential individuals in the genre of Southern Gospel Music. He has also written songs that have been widely used in other areas of Christian music—contemporary, gospel, and traditional.

A long time ago, Mosie declared, "I'm trying to do something in God's kingdom that will help someone and bring honor to God." Although an admittedly reluctant speaker, he was ordained as a Southern Baptist minister in 1970.

One of his musical masterpieces is the subject of this story. Following is the account of the writing of "Then I Met the Master."

"'Then I Met the Master' has been such a comfort to so many people, and at the same time, kind of a challenge. At first I didn't realize it was going to be that. I wrote it because I wanted to describe what happened to Jesus' disciples. They were living one kind of life before they met Him. Then after they met Him and knew Him, they lived a completely different kind of life. That's what I wanted to say.

"Once I got into the writing of the song, I realized it was getting emotional—and a lot of my songs are emotional; that's the way I am. I try to say what is true and right, and I try to say it in an original manner, using some phrases that haven't been used a great deal.

"So I began by comparing my former state with a blind man who cannot see, and with a baby who is more or less helpless; then saying that all things were different after I met Him, because after I met Him, I realized that I completely belong to Him.

"There is a sad yet beautiful story that I heard just a few years ago. A young teenager in Bradenton, Florida, passed from this life to the next singing this song. When I heard that story, I absolutely wept. I don't know which phrase she sung, but I was glad that my song was a comfort to her. I felt she might have been clinging to the last phrase, 'now I belong to Him' . . . because she really did.

"This song has also been instrumental in causing some people to commit their lives to the Lord and causing some to answer the call to preach. It has just been used in many marvelous ways. God has taken it and done far more than I ever thought could happen."

At age eighty-one, Lister still lives in central Florida, writing his music and influencing Christians in all parts of the world. Thousands of Southern Gospel singers continue to keep something in their repertoire by Mosie Lister.

Reflection

Just like Mosie, you and I can rejoice when we look back over our accomplishments and see that they helped someone along life's way, to the glory of God. "If any man minister, let him do it as of the ability which God giveth: that God in all things may be glorified through Jesus Christ, to whom be praise and dominion for ever and ever. Amen" (1 Peter 4:11).

19

It Started on a Keyboard Made of Paper

The Blood Will Never Lose Its Power

1 Peter 1:13–25

*Forasmuch as ye know that ye were not redeemed
with corruptible things, as silver and gold, from
you vain conversation received by tradition from
your fathers; but with the precious blood of Christ,
as of a lamb without blemish and without spot.*

*A*ndrae Crouch wears many hats—singer, musician, composer, and pastor, just to name a few. He presently leads the ministry of the New Christ Memorial Church in Los Angeles, California. His compositions have cut a wide path across Christianity for many years and have influenced several categories of sacred music.

Andrae and his twin sister, Sandra, were born in Los Angeles into a dedicated Christian home. His dad, Ben Crouch, at that time a lay preacher, saw to it that his family was always active in Christian ministry. While young Andrae was growing up, the family attended the Emmanuel Church of God in Christ, pastored by Rev. Samuel M. Crouch, Andrae's great-uncle, with a congregation of approximately two thousand people.

Andrae told me, "My parents had two dry-cleaning establishments; Dad managed one and Mom the other. When the opportunity presented itself, they shared their faith with those who frequented their businesses. I grew up in that kind of environment, where we were always aware of the blessings of the Lord and wanted to win souls for Him."

One day the call came to Andrae's father to preach at Macedonia Church, a small congregation about sixty miles from Los Angeles. "We had never heard my dad preach in a church—on street corners, in hospitals, and in other places—but not in a real pulpit in a church. Mom packed us a lunch and we all loaded into the car, my sister, my older brother, my parents and I, and headed off to hear Daddy preach. I remember that Mom put the lunch in the trunk of the car, including the Jell-O, which was like Kool-Aid when lunchtime came. After the service we all said, 'Ooh Daddy, you really preached!'

"My dad had been urged to preach at this little church on an interim basis, until they could secure a pastor. He was hesitant to do so but began to bargain with the Lord, 'If You will give Andrae the gift of playing the piano, I will be a full-time minister and figure out some other way to provide for my family.' I was dyslexic and stuttered very badly, so my dad knew that I wasn't a speaker, but maybe music was in me somewhere. He thought that there was not much chance of that prayer being answered and maybe he would not have to pastor that little church.

"During that first service, my dad had called me up from the audience and asked, 'Andrae, if God gave you music, would you use it for His glory in your life?' I was only eleven years old and had never thought about it. There were no musicians in our immediate or extended family. I wouldn't have been more shocked if he had asked, 'Would you like to be an astronaut?' Well, my mother believed so strongly in my dad's prayers that she went to a music store and bought a cardboard piano keyboard for me to practice fingering on. When she first showed it to me, she had placed it on top of a sewing machine stand at the dry-cleaning store. I immediately began to bang on the keyboard, pretending to play music that I had heard on the radio.

"Three weeks later, during a service in that little church, as we were about to sing 'What a Friend We Have in Jesus,' my dad called out to me, 'Andrae, come up here.' He motioned to an upright piano nearby and said, 'Okay, if you're gonna play, play.' I said to myself, *'What?'* He even took the time to show me the soft pedal and the expression pedal—I haven't to this day figured out what the middle pedal is for. When the congregation began to sing, I found the right key and began to play with both hands! About two weeks later, my father gave up his business and that was the beginning of the ministry of our entire family."

When I asked Andrae Crouch to give me the story behind his song "The Blood Will Never Lose Its Power," he told me an incredible story:

"I was only fourteen years of age, three years following my initiation to the piano, and had been invited to a friend's home. It was Memorial Day and there was to be a party with most of the guests being choir members. When I arrived, the people were in the backyard barbecuing and generally having a good time. I was so shy and little—I was only four feet, eleven inches tall until I was sixteen—I didn't want to go out there. I had seen some of them with cigarettes in their hands and generally acting in ways that were not Christlike. I didn't understand that and was so disappointed I began to weep.

"I then said to the Lord, 'God, I really love You. How can this be? I would love to write songs for You. If You would give me a song, I will live for You forever.' There was a large piano in the living room and I began to play. The group in the backyard couldn't hear me. I then glanced toward the crowd and saw something that made time, it seemed, go into slow motion. I watched as they slowly poured red sauce onto the meat they were cooking. I couldn't hear for a few moments.

"Suddenly, in my mind's eye I could see Jesus carrying His cross up to Calvary, and I saw His blood. I saw people following Him up the hill where He was to be crucified. As I saw this scene, which had been prompted by the activities in the backyard, I said, 'Oh, the blood!' I then turned to my friend Billy Preston, who is also a pianist, and said, 'Play these chords.' And I began to sing, 'The blood that Jesus shed for me. . . .' The people in the backyard heard me singing and came into the house. They began to weep as they came and joined in my song. We sang for about an hour and a half. That was the writing of my first song, 'The Blood Will Never Lose Its Power.'"

After interviewing songwriters for more than four decades and researching the history of our Christian songs, I have come to realize that only a few individuals have made a greater contribution than Andrae Crouch to the singing of church folks across America.

Reflection

After multiplied thousands of men were crucified, over a period of nearly one thousand years, the only One who died in this manner and then rose again is the One who has redeemed you and me—our Lord and Savior, Jesus Christ. Thank Him today for His precious blood, the blood that daily has the power to take away our sins—blood that will never lose its power.

20

Leaving This World

Goodby, World, Goodby

1 Thessalonians 4:13–18

*Then we which are alive and remain shall be
caught up together with them in the clouds, to meet
the Lord in the air: and so shall we ever be with the
Lord.*

In a recent interview, Mosie Lister said to me, "I want to tell
you something that I have not previously shared in interviews
like this. I grew up on a farm. As a child I would walk around
the fields and in my mind I could hear choirs singing and orchestras playing. I wanted so much to write songs that those
choirs would sing and the orchestras would play. I prayed, 'God,
I'd like to be a songwriter.' I prayed that prayer for a whole
year."

Well, God began to answer that prayer when Mosie was
only eighteen years old. He confessed, "I am so amazed at
what God has allowed me to do. I thank Him and appreciate
His blessings."

Along the way he took good advice from men like Adger M.
Pace, who told him, "Be sure the tune can be whistled," and
from Jake Hess, who passed along this comment: "If you want
your songs to live, write things that are eternally true, and people
will not forget them."

I once heard someone ask, "Who is the most significant contributor of songs to the field of Southern Gospel Music?" The answer came, "You mean other than Mosie Lister?"

Mosie has been writing songs for God's people for more than fifty years. He gave his heart and life to Christ at age seventeen and began to write songs soon thereafter. He was born in 1921, in the town of Cochran, Georgia, and grew up in a very musical home, studying piano, violin, and guitar for several years. After a tour of duty in the navy, he formed a group called the Melody Masters. From that group he moved on to the legendary Statesmen, as a singer, songwriter, and arranger.

Mosie Lister thought it would be good to write a cheery song about heaven—the part about leaving this world. A great portion of the Southern Gospel classics are songs about heaven or the cross of Christ. Some time ago, Mosie told this story:

"In 1955, I just wanted to write a happy song about a Christian soul departing this world for the next one." He wrote such a song and showed it to the Statesmen Quartet, but they seemed to think it too plain and ordinary.

Mosie said, "A few days later, I wrote an up-tempo arrangement of it that I felt expressed what the song was all about. The Statesmen ran through it and fell in love with it. It worked for them."

"Goodby, World, Goodby" went on to become a standard in the Southern Gospel Music genre. For the next thirty-seven years, it was one of the most famous Christian songs in America and was recorded by thousands of Southern Gospel singers.

Mosie continued, "In 1992, through the efforts of Bill Gaither, a new Statesmen Quartet was born, and they recorded 'Goodby, World, Goodby' as the first song on their first album. It sounded so much like the original version it was downright eerie. When I first heard them sing it, I thought, 'My goodness, that's the old Statesmen all over again!' But of course, it wasn't. Hovie Lister [no relation to Mosie] was playing the piano and Jake Hess was singing the melody, with other voices working with them. That made it successful. They had very nearly recaptured that old sound, thanks to the genius of Bill Gaither."

Reflection

It should be the goal of every Christian to be able to leave this world with no regrets for the life they lived on earth—with everything under the blood of Christ.

21

Lincoln in Ebony

We'll Understand It Better By and By

1 Corinthians 13:10–13

*Now we see through a glass, darkly; but then face to
face: now I know in part; but then shall I know
even as also I am known.*

On September 14, 2002, sixty-nine years after the death of
Charles A. Tindley, who is often called a founding father of
American gospel music, a marble stone was placed in a community cemetery in the suburban town of Collingdale, Pennsylvania, near Philadelphia. The six-foot monument was placed at
Tindley's grave by a group of pastors led by the Rev. Dr. William B. McClain, senior pastor of Tindley Temple United Methodist Church, a major church in the City of Brotherly Love.
Charles Tindley was born near Berlin, Maryland, in July of 1851,
the son of a slave, Albert Tindley, and a freewoman, Hester
Miller Tindley. Hester passed away when Charles was only four,
and a year later he was separated from his father. When he
became old enough to work, he was hired out to work with
slaves, although his status as "freeborn" was recognized. Little
did the people of Berlin realize that a theological and musical
giant was springing up in their midst.

God had placed within Tindley a desire to excel, and by age
seventeen he had taught himself to read and write. At this young

age he married Daisy Henry, who bore him eight children, several of whom would later show some musical ability. The young Tindley family moved to Philadelphia where Charles obtained a job as a hod carrier, conveying mortar and other supplies to bricklayers. He later became a custodian of the John Wesley Methodist Episcopal Church, a church that was to play a major role in his life.

He attended night school for a time, and because he felt called of God to preach, he enrolled in a correspondence course from Boston School of Theology. Along with his other courses, he studied New Testament Greek. He also found a Jewish rabbi in Philadelphia who would tutor him in the study of Hebrew. In 1902, after finishing his educational ventures and pastoring several churches in Philadelphia, he became pastor of the church where he had served as janitor twenty-five years earlier.

The church experienced rapid growth and by 1906 had a congregation of five thousand members. Tindley was a tall, imposing preacher of the gospel, whose sermons reflected his study and attention to a quality ministry. He was an eloquent speaker who was heard enthusiastically by people of all races. In the early 1920s, the church, which by that time had ten thousand members, built a new sanctuary that seated thirty-two hundred worshipers. Over Tindley's protest, the congregation named the new church the Tindley Temple United Methodist Church. Tindley also became a leader within the denomination. His wife, Daisy, passed away in 1924, the very day the congregation entered the new sanctuary for the first time. Three years later, Tindley remarried.

Music played a major role throughout Charles Tindley's life. It is said that during his preaching he would often break into song, allowing the congregation to join him on the chorus. He composed gospel songs in his mind, and not having the ability to put them on paper, would dictate them to a transcriber. Often he would hold several songs in his mind before having them put on paper.

C. Austin Miles, who composed "In the Garden," published eight of Tindley's songs in his *New Songs of the Gospel* in 1901. Over the next twenty-five years, Tindley himself published thirty-four additional songs. A later book, *Soul Echoes: A Collection of Songs for Religious Meetings,* contained many of his musical offerings. Tindley and his sons formed the Paradise Publishing Company, which first published *New Songs of Paradise!* volume 1. Volume 6 of the series contained all of Tindley's works.

"We'll Understand It Better By and By" is one of several C. A. Tindley songs that found their way into the hymnals and then into the repertoire of a host of Southern Gospel Music touring groups. It is still being sung to this day. A host of musicians owe a debt to Charles Tindley—including, by his own admission, Thomas A. Dorsey, author of "Precious Lord, Take My Hand." Many have called Tindley and Dorsey the fathers of gospel music. Other Tindley songs that have stood the test of time include "Nothing Between (My Soul and the Savior)," "Stand by Me," and "Leave It There." One Tindley song, "I'll Overcome Some Day," written in 1901, gave rise to the popular civil rights song "We Shall Overcome," although more in reflection and concept than in actual words or tune.

Dr. McClain, professor of preaching and worship at Wesley Theological Seminary in Washington, D.C., has helped disseminate the music of C. A. Tindley. In 1980, he created *Songs of Zion,* published by Abingdon Press, which included approximately sixteen songs by Tindley, and sold more than 1.2 million copies.

Tindley died in 1933, at the age of eighty-two. Thousands in Philadelphia felt the loss and went into mourning. It is reported that approximately five thousand people crowded into the church, which seated only thirty-two hundred, to hear the memorial tributes to this spiritual giant. Some had openly recognized him as a "Lincoln in Ebony."

When thumbing through various hymnals, you will often find, among other songs by Charles A. Tindley, "We'll Understand It Better By and By":

We are often tossed and driv'n on the restless sea of time,
Sombre skies and howling tempest oft succeed a bright
   sunshine,
In the land of perfect day, when the mists have rolled away,
We will understand it better by and by.

Chorus:
By and by when the morning comes,
When the saints of God are gathered home,
We'll tell the story how we've overcome,
For we'll understand it better by and by.

Trials dark on every hand, and we cannot understand,
All the ways that God would lead us to that blessed
   promised land,
But He'll guide us with His eye and we'll follow till we die,
For we'll understand it better by and by.

Tindley Temple United Methodist Church is on the "tour of historic sites" in Philadelphia, allowing many visitors each year to see the famed edifice. Tindley's study is still intact with memorabilia and displays of his writings, books, programs, and correspondence.

Reflection

Tindley seemed to write for suffering people. In most of his songs there is a great anticipation of heaven, when the trials of God's people will finally be over. He could have been writing for millions of people in our day and age.

22

Lord, I Don't Even Have a Title!

His Hand in Mine

John 10:22–30

*My Father, which gave them me, is greater than all;
and no man is able to pluck them out of my
Father's hand.*

𝓜osie Lister had the good fortune of growing up in a musical home. Very early in life it was evident that he was going to be a man of music. Yet there was little indication in those early years that he would grow up to be one of the most influential writers ever of Southern Gospel Music.

When Mosie was twenty years old, he was offered a singing position with the Sunny South Quartet. It was a wonderful opportunity, but he would quickly declare that he would much rather write music than sing. Writing music was a dream that went back to his boyhood.

His years in the navy did not lessen his desire to write music and to be involved in its presentation to Southern Gospel fans. Shortly after his discharge from military duty, Mosie was instrumental in forming a group called the Melody Masters. This launched him into a music career, the result of which was that he helped chart the direction of Southern Gospel Music for many years. A major reason for his influence was his association with the famed Statesmen Quartet, both as a singer and as an arranger.

Hovie Lister, for years the leader of the Statesmen Quartet, said, "I give him credit for molding the style and sound of the Statesmen." Whether as a singer or arranger, Mosie's interaction with that group helped to boost their popularity. He often wrote songs especially for the Statesmen, and particularly for Big Chief Weatherington and Jake Hess, singers in the group.

Several years later, in 1953, Mosie penned one of his greatest masterpieces. In his own words, here's how "His Hand in Mine" came into being:

"One day I was casually playing on the piano, just going from one chord to the next and creating little melodies. I wasn't trying to write anything, just having a little fun in my own mind with my limited keyboard ability. After a bit, I found myself playing what became the melody for a song I would later write.

"I played it all the way through and then repeated the whole thing. It stuck in my mind, and for a year every time I sat down to play the piano, I would automatically start playing that little melody. It was easy to play, and it fit my hand. I liked it, but I didn't have any words for it. I wondered if I could write lyrics for it, and for a time I couldn't come up with a single idea.

"One day while returning from a town about seventy miles southwest of Atlanta, I started thinking about the fact that I just couldn't write words to that melody. I suddenly remembered an old pastor friend of mine who often stated that we ought to talk to God, at times, like we would talk to a friend or an older brother. He said that we should use plain, everyday English and just say exactly what we feel at the time. I thought, 'That's what I'll do.'

"I stopped the car by the side of the road and said, 'Lord, I hope You are listening, and I believe You are. I have this melody, and I've been trying to write words for it and just don't have anything as yet. I have no idea what to say in the song. I don't even have a title; I don't have a single word. If it is Your will for this song to be written, I ask You to write it for me, because I simply cannot do it in my own strength. I give up. If You want it written, just write it. Tell me the words, and I'll write them down.'

"I started the car again and drove home. By the time I reached our house, I had all of the lyrics in my mind, title and all. I went into the house and took my guitar and played it. I sang it to my wife, and she loved it. There were a couple of places in the song that bothered me, so I didn't show the song to anyone else for several weeks. I eventually rewrote the beginning of the chorus, but otherwise I didn't change a thing.

"I soon showed it to some friends who were professional singers and asked them to try it and let me know what they thought. My impression was that it didn't excite a single person.

"After about a year, a couple of singing groups finally recorded it but nothing special happened to it. A few years later, a new singer on the scene by the name of Elvis Presley recorded it. It became the title of his first gospel album. I had no idea he even knew the song, but since his recording of it, 'His Hand in Mine' has been established as a standard in Christian music."

Reflection

Isn't it magnificent how God wants to take over when we come to the end of our own way? And He always makes it turn out right.

23

On a Bus Heading West

I'm Standing on the Solid Rock
and
Touring That City

Psalm 31:1–8

*For thou art my rock and my fortress; therefore for
thy name's sake lead me, and guide me.*

When calling the roll of those who have been in the forefront of the world of Southern Gospel Music, Harold Lane, a
veteran singer and songwriter, is not the first name mentioned.
Nevertheless, his popular songs have been recorded and sung
by thousands and heard by millions. For many years, Lane's
songs have appeared in songbooks and choral arrangements,
as well as on television, radio, cassette tapes, videos, and com-
pact discs.

Lane, born in 1929 in Huntington, West Virginia, started his
music training in high school playing trombone in the band.
He became a Christian while attending Marshall University in
Huntington, where he continued his music education. He later
became a high school band director and music teacher at Wayne
High School in Wayne, West Virginia.

At age thirty-seven, he joined the Speer Family, one of the
most famous of all the Southern Gospel Music touring groups.

G. T. "Dad" Speer, a native of Double Springs, Alabama, began the first Speer quartet more than eighty years ago. They broke a major barrier in this genre of music by including female voices in a field totally dominated by all-male quartets. For twenty-two years, Harold Lane was part of the success of this group, which recorded more than seventy albums, five of which received Grammy Award nominations. The Speer Family received eight Dove Awards for Best Mixed Group of the Year. Twice they received Dove Awards for Best Album of the Year, and four times, consecutively, for Best Female Vocalist of the Year. In 1996, they were awarded the Alabama Music Hall of Fame Life Work Award for Performing Achievement.

In the late 1970s, the Speer Family was on their bus traveling to another engagement, "probably to California," according to Lane, who had joined the group a few years earlier. As they rode along, Lane fell to thinking of his son back home who was "messed up in the drug scene." His thoughts quickly turned to the One who can solve drug problems, or any other problem for that matter, and how Christians who trust in the Lord are standing on a firm foundation, Jesus Christ the Chief Cornerstone. Another musician, the psalmist David, declares, "He brought me up also out of an horrible pit, out of the miry clay, and set my feet upon a rock, and established my goings. And he hath put a new song in my mouth, even praise unto our God" (Psalm 40:2–3).

As Lane rode along, verses began to take shape in his mind and along with them came a melody. Calling on his college music training, he took music paper and put "I'm Standing on the Solid Rock" in manuscript form. From there it has made its way into every nook and cranny of the Southern Gospel Music world.

In the song, Lane reminds us that through our disappointments, strife, and discontentment, we can cast our every care on our Savior. In the chorus he tells us that we are safe from the storms that rage around us, and that we have untold wealth in our relationship to Jesus.

Another one of Harold Lane's songs that has reached great heights is a song written in the home of Ben Speer after a Speer Family practice session. Harold Lane said, "During the session, a friend of the Speer family, from North Carolina, came by to visit Mom Speer, who was seriously ill with cancer. As he was leaving, he turned to me and said, 'If I don't see you again, you will find me touring that City.' That thought stayed with me, and a few days later I wrote the song, 'Touring That City.'

"While participating in the *Gospel Singing Jubilee*, a television show, we met up with the Inspirations, a singing group from Bryson City, North Carolina, who were searching for two additional songs to include on a record project. Ben Speer and one of the lady members of the Speer Family helped me to sing 'Touring That City' for them. They liked it and sang it on a television program the very next day." And so, another Harold Lane song was launched. Many other singing groups have helped to popularize it.

In that song, Lane shares the message that as we tour the City of God we will find a place of pretty streets made of gold, and Jesus our Savior who gave us the victory will be there with us forever. Even though we have burdens and problems on this earth, all will be made right when we reach that City.

Harold Lane and his wife, Betty, live in Nashville, where they attend the Church of Christ, and Harold occasionally writes music. To date he has penned almost ninety Southern Gospel songs. He delights in going to the National Quartet Convention held each year in Louisville, Kentucky, where he can renew fellowship with a great host of singers who have become his friends through the years.

Reflection

As Christians, and especially during times of testing, we take great solace in the truth that we indeed are standing on a firm foundation, the solid Rock of our salvation, Jesus Christ.

24

Out of the Darkness, a Sunbeam

He Looked Beyond My Fault and Saw My Need

Ephesians 2:1–10

But God, who is rich in mercy, for his great love
wherewith he loved us, even when we were dead in
sins, hath quickened us together with Christ, (by
grace ye are saved.)

I shall never forget my interviews with Dottie Rambo, a gracious soul who gladly shared the stories behind her wonderful songs. To date she has penned approximately twenty-five hundred songs, many of which are standards and classics. Some people have even compared her to the great Fanny Crosby, who wrote so many of the songs we have sung in church for years—songs such as "Blessed Assurance," "Rescue the Perishing," and "To God Be the Glory," to name a few.

Dottie started her songwriting and singing career as a mere child. She was married at age sixteen and a year and a half later became a mother when Reba was born. By age three, Reba was singing with her famous parents.

During Reba's early, formative years, Dottie had to leave her in the care of others in order to travel to distant cities to sing in concerts and for church meetings. That was especially difficult for Dottie, who later confessed that she had desperately wanted to be there to help Reba with school chores, be a part of the

PTA, and to do all of the things mothers do for their children. To put it in her words, "It was torture" not to be able to do those things.

The day finally came when Reba was happily made a part of the family trio, the Rambos. They became very famous with their recordings and concerts. Dottie played a part on seventy albums of songs, either with the family group or as a soloist.

Thousands of singers have recorded her music—the very famous, the nearly famous, and multitudes of others who have great aspirations. Some of the famous include Whitney Houston, Elvis Presley, George Beverly Shea, Sandi Patti, and Barbara Mandrell.

Many awards and recognitions have come her way, including numerous Grammy and Dove Awards. She was named Songwriter of the Century by the Christian Country Music Association, and is now a member of the Gospel Music Hall of Fame and the Southern Gospel Music Hall of Fame.

A crushing sorrow in Dottie Rambo's life gave birth to her most famous song. Following is her own story as she related it to me:

"My brother was a sinner boy. He had never been a Christian, but he and I were very close. We double-dated when we were young, although he was two years older. He would always come to hear me sing but would leave before the invitation of the service.

"During the time I was writing this particular song, Eddy was dying with cancer. He had become a very wicked boy, but I loved him very much. So, I went to the hospital to see him. They had brought him to Nashville to die. I went into the room, a ward that he shared with another man. I pulled the curtain around his bed and sat down and began to talk to him. I said, 'Darling, the doctors say unless a miracle happens, or unless this drug works, you have only about five or six weeks to live.'

"None of my family would tell him. I knew he was lost, and I decided along with my mother that I must level with him. He began to cry and said, 'But, Sis, I've been so wicked. I've been in prison. I've been a gambler and a thief and everything that goes along with all of that. I am just too wicked for God to save me.' I started witnessing to Eddy and praying with him. But he could find no peace.

"A few days later, as I sat alone in a rocking chair in my living room at home praying for Eddy, the Lord impressed on me that He wanted to give me some words for Eddy. The lyrics began to come.

"I went back to the hospital to visit Eddy and said, 'Darling, I have some words for you.' [By then she had the melody, an old English tune.] I stood over his bed and looked down on my brother who, by this time, weighed only sixty-five pounds. I started to sing 'Amazing grace shall always be my song of praise.' He started to weep and wanted me to write the words down. I did so and left them with him.

"A few days later, I went to Cleveland, Tennessee, to sing in a Baptist church. I asked them to pray for Eddy. Following the music, at about eleven o'clock, the minister began to speak. I thought of Eddy, but the tears were not there. All of a sudden, I sensed that Eddy was fine. A beautiful peace came over me. The Lord just seemed to let me know that Eddy was okay.

"The next day, I returned to Nashville and went to see Eddy, but they had taken him home to spend his final days. I walked into his room and said, 'I have some good news. I want to tell you something.' He said, 'Sis, before you do, I want to tell you something. Yesterday at about eleven o'clock, I really found my peace with God.'

"The Lord had really saved him. My song became alive to me. I realized what God had done. I began to tell Eddy about love and what the love of God had done. God's love is so far beyond us. I told him about the thief on the cross beside Jesus, who was saved and had no chance to have a personal testimony or even to be baptized. Yet Jesus said to him, 'This day thou shalt be with me in Paradise.'"

To this day, in spite of ten back surgeries and enormous bouts with pain, Dottie Rambo continues to crisscross the nation, singing for the Savior. She states on her Web site, "These are wonderful blessings from the great Lord above, and I owe everything back to Him. My daily goal in life is to serve Him and share with the many hurting and wounded people in this world the wonderful message of God's great and unconditional love."

Reflection

In spite of all we do, no matter how hard we try, we can never understand why the Lord would love us so—why He would express it and show it to us in so many ways. "But God commendeth his love toward us, in that, while we were yet sinners, Christ died for us" (Romans 5:8).

25

Singing for Gypsy Smith

Love Grew Where the Blood Fell

Isaiah 53:1–11

But he was wounded for our transgressions, he was bruised for our iniquities: the chastisement of our peace was upon him; and with his stripes we are healed.

The crowds had gathered at the massive Soldier Field in Chicago, in 1943, to hear the famed evangelist Gypsy Smith, the British preacher who was born in a tent and raised in a Gypsy camp near London. In his early years, Rodney Smith was an officer in the Salvation Army, which he joined at age seventeen, just one year after his conversion. He was now eighty-two years old, and his travels had carried him to many parts of the world—from small churches in rural areas, to a Paris opera house, and now to a giant stadium, giving his message of salvation to many thousands of people. This stop in the Windy City was one of more than thirty trips to the United States. Smith died on the *Queen Mary* in 1947, attempting one more venture to America.

On this particular night in Soldier Field, before Smith was to speak, a five-year-old lad was helped to the platform to sing "God Bless America." His name was John Stallings, and he would later become a talented singer, songwriter, pastor, and evangelist.

His songs would one day be sung by such notable singers as George Beverly Shea, the Billy Graham Crusade Choir, Kenneth Copeland, Jeannie C. Riley, and Bill Gaither, just to name a few.

Young John was saved under the ministry of his father, J. Marvin Stallings, then pastor of Beverly Hills Baptist Church in Jacksonville, Florida. Through the influence of his mother, Onivia, he began taking piano lessons at age ten, but he soon gave up the piano as his main instrument in favor of the guitar. By the time John was sixteen, his family had moved to Orlando, Florida, where he started his songwriting ventures. To date, he has written approximately 180 songs, about fifty of which have been published or recorded. In 1977, one of his most famous songs, "Learning to Lean," won a Dove Award, the Singing News Award, and the Quartet Convention Award, a feat no other song has accomplished. Stallings told me the following story about another of his songs, "Love Grew Where the Blood Fell," which has touched the lives of thousands, if not millions of people, and which seems to be rediscovered from time to time.

"I was the pastor of First Assembly of God Church, in Montgomery, Alabama, from 1971 to 1975. During the latter part of my ministry there, I preached a five-week series of sermons on the blood of Christ. During the final sermon, I referred to a passage of Scripture, 1 Corinthians 2:7–8: 'But we speak the wisdom of God in a mystery, even the hidden wisdom, which God ordained before the world unto our glory: Which none of the princes of this world knew: for had they known it, they would not have crucified the Lord of glory.'

"To me, what this passage is really saying is that Satan caused men to do something that turned out to be the exact opposite of what he wanted to accomplish. That was the biggest mistake he ever made. He was not aware of what the consequences would mean. (As early as Genesis 3:15 God said, 'And I will put enmity between thee and the woman, and between thy seed and her seed; it shall bruise thy head, and thou shalt bruise his heel.') As far as Satan was concerned, he had won a great victory, but in reality it meant his ultimate defeat (the bruising of his head) and a victory for millions of Christians—a triumph of greater magnitude than we can ever imagine. The shedding of Jesus' blood was payment for the sins of the whole world— redemption and salvation for man.

"A few days after the last sermon in the series, I was at home relaxing a bit, playing the piano, when again thoughts of Christ's crucifixion began running through my mind. Before I quite realized it, I had a song. It needed very little changing after I had written it. It seemed as if I was holding the pen and the Lord was putting the words on paper. It was like taking dictation.

"In the chorus of the song, I say, 'Love grew where the blood fell, flowers of hope sprang up for men in misery. Sin died where the blood fell, and I'm so glad this precious blood has covered me.'

"In the first verse of the song, I speak of seeing my Jesus on the cross, and people around are crying, looking on. A man would think it tragedy, but the victory that the world couldn't see was when they nailed him to that tree, he would break the chains of sin and set men free. My inspiration came from those verses in the second chapter of 1 Corinthians."

Sometime later, John was in Nashville where he visited the Vincent Studio and chanced upon Brock Speer of the famed Speer Family. John shared his song with him and Speer liked it so much his family group recorded it, thus launching "Love Grew Where the Blood Fell" into the genre of Southern Gospel Music.

In this song, John Stallings rose to great heights in his use of the English language to express scriptural truth. Somewhat obscured in the song, though not intentionally, are the stark realities of crucifixion—there have been few methods of execution more torturous or more excruciatingly painful—and the Romans had mastered it. As we examine the process of execution, we have a better glimpse of the magnitude of the love of God.

By design, death on a cross was not a brief experience. No vital organs were damaged, so it was a slow, agonizing demise. Crucifixion was used as a means of execution for nearly one thousand years, beginning about 600 B.C. It wasn't until A.D. 337 that crucifixion was banned in Rome, out of reverence for Christ's death, by the Christian emperor Constantine the Great.

Christ took the cross, a tool of death and humiliation, and made it a badge of honor. Today, we proudly wear crosses on our clothing or put them on the front of our churches or in other noticeable places—but it was not always so.

John Stallings took this meaningful subject and gave to the world a song that draws men to Christ, the One who so willingly gave His life in the manner described in this story. John and his wife, Juda, continue to travel—preaching, singing, and writing songs.

Reflection

When Jesus said, "It is finished," while still on the cross, He meant that the blood flow could be concluded. There would be no more need for innocent animals to be sacrificed to atone for your sins or mine. Our salvation has been paid for—in full!

26

Singing in the Forest

He's Still Working on Me

Psalm 139:1–14

I will praise thee; for I am fearfully and wonderfully made: marvellous are thy works; and that my soul knoweth right well.

*H*undreds of songs have had very strange beginnings, but perhaps none more unusual than "He's Still Working on Me." One has only to read the lyrics to understand why the song works for people of all ages. Children love it as well as senior adults, chiefly because we never get to the place where God is not "working on us," trying to shape us and conform us to the image of His Son (Romans 8:29).

Joel Hemphill was born in Fresno, California, the tenth of fourteen children born into a preacher's home. Joel said, "My dad was an old-time preacher who preached for sixty-eight years. He sang a lot—when he was happy, when he was sad, when he was lonely, in church and at home, he just sang. He taught all of his children to love Southern Gospel Music. When I turned sixteen, I began to take music more seriously and learned to play the guitar."

By age twenty-one, Joel was the pastor of a Pentecostal church in a small paper-mill town of fourteen thousand people in Louisiana. He led that church for ten years. During that time, he often prayed that God would see fit to give them a greater ministry in order that they might reach more souls for Christ and touch more lives. He told me, "I was troubled in my spirit, and I told my wife, LeBreeska, that I was afraid we were going to grow old in this little town and will not have affected many people for God.

"We set aside days of fasting and prayer, bringing the burden of our hearts before the Lord. As a result, the Lord gave me a gift—the gift of songwriting.

"Although LeBreeska and I had been singing together for years, I never aspired to be a songwriter. Almost from the beginning of my songwriting ventures, Southern Gospel singing groups began to sing and record my songs." As their children, Joey, Trent, and Candy, became old enough, they joined their parents in the family group, the Singing Hemphills.

Joel related the following story. "I was driving our bus one night when 'He's Still Working on Me' began to come into being. I often become fascinated with church marquees, bumper stickers, and other places where short messages are posted. On this particular night I saw a bumper sticker that read, 'Please be patient, God is not finished with me yet.' It impacted me because it reminded me that we are not all in the same grade; none of us are finished works of God.

"About a month later I was engaged in one of my favorite sports—deer hunting. I was out in the woods enjoying what deer hunters do, waiting for a deer to come near. While sitting there, I greatly enjoyed being in God's creation, watching the birds, squirrels, and other small animals. Presently my thoughts were turned to 'creation week' when God made the world and all of His marvelous handiwork. I then thought of that bumper sticker. I had filed it away in my mind as I have so often done when I saw things that I thought might be useful at a later time.

"The message on the bumper sticker, 'God is not finished with me yet,' gave rise to a song that suddenly came out as 'He's still workin' on me, to make me what I ought to be.' The song was born right there in the woods, waiting for a deer."

This unusual crossover song was soon in the number one position on the *Singing News* charts, where it stayed for three months. It was nominated at least three different times for Song of the Year and nominated for a Dove Award several years in a row. In the song, Hemphill says that we should all have a sign on our hearts, asking all who observe us to not judge us now but to wait until God has perfected us. We are fashioned by our Father's loving hand.

Over the past three decades or more, the name Hemphill is one of the most recognized names in the world of Southern Gospel Music. The family group has received six Dove Awards and Joel has been nominated ten times by the Gospel Music Association as Songwriter of the Year. Hemphill songs have been used by such outstanding artists as the Cathedrals and the Gaither Vocal Band. The Hemphill children have gone on to other pursuits, and Joel and LeBreeska are now joined by David Hall, who sings the third part and plays keyboard. They have, on a number of occasions, appeared in the Gaither Homecoming concerts and on the videos. In addition, they sing all over the world.

Reflection

In order for us to be the "workmanship" of Christ that brings honor to Him, we must draw close to Him every morning and throughout the day never wander farther away than His fingertips.

27

Sleeping on the Front Seats

*What a Beautiful Day for
the Lord to Come Again!*

Matthew 24:27–31

*And they shall see the Son of man coming in the
clouds of heaven with power and great glory.*

*M*ultitalented Aaron Wilburn is one of the most recognizable names in Southern Gospel Music. He is equally at home playing rhythm guitar, writing songs, emceeing a Southern Gospel concert or an awards presentation, or just making an audience laugh. Aaron has written more than eight hundred songs, with an astounding 75 percent of them published or recorded.

Aaron was born to Eugene and Lola Wilburn in 1950 in Ardmore, Alabama. He was one of seven children, and theirs was a musical family, often singing at their local Free Will Baptist Church.

J. Otis King looked a little like Colonel Sanders in his white suit and string bow tie, with his gray hair and goatee, but he was a "fireball of a Southern Baptist preacher," according to Aaron. He came to Huntsville, Alabama, to preach in a tent revival when Aaron was only thirteen. One night, following the evangelist's sermon, young Wilburn "hit the sawdust trail" and gave his heart and life to Jesus Christ.

Aaron began his musical ventures using a fourteen dollar guitar, bought with money he made by picking cotton. Two years later, he wrote his first song, "Modern Age of Progress," which was recorded by the famed Sego Brothers and Naomi—a formidable start for one so young. He has continued from that promising debut to greatly influence Southern Gospel Music.

During an interview a few years ago, I asked Aaron to tell me exactly how he came to write "What a Beautiful Day for the Lord to Come Again!" I'm sure you will enjoy the story as much as I have:

"I was traveling with the Happy Goodman Family as a rhythm guitar player, and I would also sing two or three songs during each of their concerts. In those years, 1973 to 1974, we were also a part of the Gospel Singing Jubilee. Vestal Goodman was having a few health problems at the time but kept a wonderful Christian attitude. She had a saying that she would occasionally repeat—actually it was a question, 'Wouldn't this be a beautiful day for the Lord to come again?'

"At the time, we were traveling on a new bus that had not been completely revamped to meet all of our needs. They were in the process of making a bed for me in Rusty Goodman's quarters. I was to share a room with him. In the meantime, I was sleeping on the front seats of the bus, because I was the only one small enough to do so. After everyone else was in bed, I would bed down up front. The next morning, I was up with whoever was up first. They would wake me as they came out of their rooms to the front of the bus.

"Early one morning, Vestal, who was in a lot of pain and unable to sleep, came to the front of the bus. She sat down by a window, and as she did so I got up and went over and sat down beside her. She pointed out the window to a cloud and asked, 'Son, do you see that cloud?' I nodded, indicating that I did see it. She then continued, 'That could be the one that He sets His foot upon.' Then she turned to me and asked, 'Wouldn't this be a beautiful day for the Lord to come again?'

"She had repeated that question from time to time onstage, on the bus, or in conversations. When she asked me the question on this particular morning, with the sun coming up, and with the beautiful clouds in the sky, it really had an impact on me. Suddenly I thought, 'What a great idea for a song!' I began working on it, actually just putting it together in my mind.

"The Happy Goodman Family was in the midst of putting a new album together. I had no idea that I would have time to finish the song for that particular album, because they were about ready to go into the studio. Rusty said, 'We still do not have the one song we need.'

"I had already shared what I was working on with Eddie Crook, their pianist. The day before the recording session, he and I got together and put the finishing touches on my song. The Goodmans recorded it the next day. The taping of the song followed their usual pattern for learning songs. Rusty learned the melody first, and by the time the group heard him sing the tune through a couple of times, they all had their parts. They then recorded it. The only thing they had in their hands were the lyrics. No music was on paper—only in Eddie Crook's head and mine. It was amazing!

"Before the recording came out, they used the song in a concert. The next morning, Eddie went into the office and said, 'We've got a monster! They sang "What a Beautiful Day for the Lord to Come Again!" and the audience wanted it repeated over and over again. The crowd began singing it with them the second time through.'

"When the song was released in 1974, it immediately went to number one on the *Singing News* charts and stayed there for thirteen months. At the concerts, the emcee would say, 'From Madisonville, Kentucky, would you make welcome the happiest people on earth, the Happy Goodman Family!' From the time the crowds would hear, 'From Madisonville, Kentucky . . .' you could scarcely make out the rest of his introduction. The audience would almost drown him out with their applause."

The song has become a favorite among Southern Gospel Music fans and will no doubt remain so until the Lord comes again!

Reflection

The next time you experience a lovely day, ask yourself, "Wouldn't this be a beautiful day for the Lord to come again?" Then answer the question honestly and with fervent consideration.

28

Songwriting on Interstate 75

Serenaded by Angels

Hebrews 12:22–29

*But ye are come unto mount Sion, and unto the
city of the living God, the heavenly Jerusalem, and
to an innumerable company of angels.*

$\mathcal{K}$irk Talley has been singing for audiences for more than twenty-five years. Although known primarily as a Southern Gospel musician, Talley has been able to cross into traditional and contemporary Christian music, making major contributions with songs such as "Triumphantly the Church Shall Rise" and "Magnify Him," to name only two.

Kirk's musical roots go back to his hometown of Whitesburg, Tennessee, where he was born into a very musical family. He related to me in an interview, "My dad taught me to sing first tenor before I could read. He was a song leader and my brother was a pianist, so we sang. When we were growing up, we sang at our little church, Shady Grove Free Will Baptist Church in Whitesburg."

Kirk told me his straightforward salvation testimony: "After the preacher had given his sermon, he gave an invitation for people to receive Christ. The Lord spoke to my heart and I knew I needed to walk the aisle and trust Christ as my Savior, and that is what I did. And you know, it was the best thing that ever happened to me."

Kirk wrote his first song, "When I See His Face," at age fifteen. Several Southern Gospel groups recorded the song, including the Hoppers, the Dixie Melody Boys, and the Cathedral Quartet.

In his early years, Kirk sang with his family group and then moved on to become the first tenor with the Hoppers, the Cathedrals, and the Talleys. On special occasions, he sings with The Trio, a group composed of Kirk, Ivan Parker, and Anthony Burger. They appear together periodically when not pursuing their solo ministries.

Kirk began his solo career in 1993 when the Talley Trio came off the road in order for Roger and Debra Talley to spend time raising their daughter, Lauren. Kirk later said, "I am really proud of Roger and Debbie for making their decision to stay closer to home and give Lauren a normal life. I think God honors those kinds of decisions." Now, after ten years have passed, Lauren has joined her parents in a family trio.

In an interview, I asked Kirk if there was a story behind the writing of his very popular song "Serenaded by Angels." Here is his response:

"Yes, I have some very good friends in North Carolina, Jamie and Deborah Parsons, whom I have known for years. Jamie was in the automobile sales business and owned several dealerships in that state. I got to know the family and to be in their home on many occasions. They were great people!

"I had traveled to Israel and was returning when I received word that Deborah had suffered a brain aneurysm and was in the hospital in a coma. My concert schedule was so full that I just didn't have the opportunity to make the trip to see them right away. During that time, I happened to be traveling on Interstate 75 when the Lord impressed upon me that Deborah was not going to recover, and that I would be asked to sing at her funeral service. The Lord seemed to speak to me about writing a special song for the occasion.

"I wrote a song that very day. At the church where I was

singing that evening, I said to the people, 'I wrote a song today and I would like to sing it for you now. I would like to know what you think about it.' The response of the people was tremendous. They all seemed to love it. During a concert the following evening, I repeated the song, with the same response from that audience. Two days later, I received word that Deborah had passed away, and so I made the trip to their hometown and sang my special song during her funeral.

"During those days, I was making plans to record another album. I called the record company and said, 'I have a song that I really need to record.' Their response was very positive and 'Serenaded by Angels' was soon being played in many places." That year, *Gospel Voice* magazine presented Kirk with three Diamond Awards: Soloist of the Year, Songwriter of the Year, and Song of the Year . . . all for "Serenaded by Angels."

Kirk continued, "'Serenaded by Angels' has been the most popular song I have ever recorded. Even now, five years later, it is still my most requested song. It's just a simple song that I never thought would amount to a whole lot, but the timing was right—plus it offers comfort to people who have lost loved ones."

Kirk continues to travel, presenting his concerts, and his beautiful tenor voice is a crowd-pleaser everywhere he goes. "I want the people to feel comfortable," he said of his concerts. "I want them to feel like they are in my living room, just having a great time, lifting up praise to our Lord."

Even when he eventually decides to retire from singing, his songs will still live in the hearts of millions of Christians. The major portion of his Christian influence, even today, is his songwriting—the blending of biblical messages with beautiful melodies. To date he has written nearly two hundred songs. To report all of the awards and recognitions that have come to Kirk and his songs would take more space than we have in this story.

Reflection

One of the great joys in heaven will be to observe the angels and their attention to our Savior and King, Jesus Christ. While we're still here on earth, it is a comfort to know that the angels of God assist Him in encouraging us.

29

The Afterthought That Became Number One

I'm Glad I Know Who Jesus Is

2 Timothy 1:1–12

*I know whom I have believed, and am persuaded
that he is able to keep that which I have committed
unto him against that day.*

In more than one case, a song has been deemed by its author as unworthy of much consideration, yet the Lord in His infinite wisdom has overruled human rationale and brought the song to a place of prominence. Such was the subject of this story. God says that He has "chosen the weak things of the world to confound the things which are mighty" (1 Corinthians 1:27).

Geron Davis was born in Bogalusa, Louisiana, in 1960, into the home of Rev. Gerald and Patricia Davis. While Geron was still a very young child, he taught himself to play the piano. He listened to recordings of his favorite singers—groups such as the Happy Goodman Family, the Rambos, and Southern Gospel quartets whose arrangements were done by Lari Goss—and tried to pick out their harmonies. Goss, the composer of the masterful "Cornerstone," was greatly influential in the young Geron's life. In an interview Geron said, "I was raised around music. My mom played piano, my dad played the guitar, and they sang together. I often sang with them, even at ages four and five. They would stand me on a piano bench behind the pulpit and I would sing the melody while Mom sang alto and Dad sang tenor and played his guitar.

"I started making up songs as a small child, simple choruses that we would sing in Sunday school. I would often sit at the piano and try to pick out tunes. During those days I was listening to a lot of music."

Geron met his wife, Becky, at college in 1981. Since their marriage, they have written and recorded numerous songs, individually and collectively, and have been recording and performing together for more than twenty years. They are also known for their outstanding choral workshops and have ministered with choirs from Christ Church, Brooklyn Tabernacle, and Prestonwood Baptist Church, just to name a few. Numerous major publishing companies have distributed their music.

A few of the hundreds who have recorded and performed their songs are the Gaither Vocal Band, Janet Paschal, the Martins, Kirk Talley, Gold City, Ivan Parker, the Cathedrals, and the Nelons. Another of Geron's songs, "Holy Ground," was used at the funeral service of President Bill Clinton's mother. Geron is seen on many of the Gaither Homecoming videos. Geron wrapped it up this way, "Becky and I have always sought to touch the lives of people with our music."

In an interview, I asked Geron to tell me the story behind the writing of "I'm Glad I Know Who Jesus Is," and he told me the following story:

"I was serving as minister of music in a large church in Alexandria, Louisiana, a church of about twenty-five hundred members with a choir of approximately 150 voices. We were making plans for our 1990 Christmas musical, a time when many people from the community would come in and enjoy the Christmas music with us. We had a great relationship with the other churches of the city.

"I had an older group of singers in the choir, a quartet of very experienced people who were loved by all of the senior adults, and I wanted to present them in some manner during the program. We called them the Oldtimers Quartet. I would, from time to time, find things that were good for them to present. In this particular program, I wanted their song to have a Southern Gospel flavor, because in that part of Louisiana you have air to breathe, food to eat, and Southern Gospel Music to listen to. Those were the staples of life.

"I wanted the Oldtimers Quartet to do something original, never heard before, and so I sat down and wrote 'I'm Glad I Know Who Jesus Is.' I literally wrote the song in fifteen minutes. I taught it to them that evening and they loved it. When they sang it during the musical, the people loved it. I really didn't know what to think of the song myself, because the Oldtimers Quartet could sing out of the phone book and people would love it.

"A month or so later, the Nelons, good friends of mine, called me and asked if I had any songs that I thought they might be interested in. They, along with the producer, Lari Goss, were searching for new songs to put into an upcoming project, and they needed a few more things to listen to and consider. I said, 'Yes, I have some songs that I can send to you.' So I sat down at the piano and recorded four songs to send to them. The last song I put on the tape, I almost didn't include: 'I'm Glad I Know Who Jesus Is.' And then, I thought, 'You know what? That song has a Southern feel, and they might like it.' So I stuck it onto the tape. I almost decided against it, but at the last minute I put it in the group.

"They recorded the song and put it on their new album. They 'singled' two or three songs from the album and sent them to radio stations, but not 'I'm Glad I Know Who Jesus Is.' Sometime later, they recorded another album and tried in the same manner to get some reaction from it. But a funny thing happened; the stations went back to the former album and began to play 'I'm Glad I Know Who Jesus Is.' The response was so great that the radio stations contacted the record company and the Nelons and said, 'We love "I'm Glad I Know Who Jesus Is." We're getting a large number of requests for it.' After hearing that, the record company went back to the former album and released my song as a single. It soon went to number one with the radio stations and was number one on the *Singing News* charts."

In this unusual song, Geron emphasizes the fact that from the birth of Jesus to this very day, the world has not known who Jesus really is. But we as Christians have come to know Him as the Alpha and the Omega, the Beginning and the End, our Counselor, our Deliverer, and our Everlasting Father.

Reflection

The goal of every Christian should be to get to know our Savior, in all of His love and mercy. We should realize afresh and anew each morning who Jesus really is, drawing close to His heart throughout the day.

30

The Death of a Quantrell Raider

I Should Have Been Crucified

Isaiah 53:1–12

*Surely he hath borne our griefs, and carried our
sorrows: yet we did esteem him stricken, smitten of
God, and afflicted. But he was wounded for our
transgressions, he was bruised for our iniquities: the
chastisement of our peace was upon him; and with
his stripes we are healed.*

*O*ver a span of two decades, the songs of Gordon Jensen have
been recorded more than two thousand times and have been
translated into fifteen languages. Among those recording the
songs are celebrated artists Cynthia Clawson, the Imperials,
Dallas Holm, the Cathedrals quartet, Doug Oldham, and
Larnelle Harris. Jensen, a quartet singer, pianist, and songwriter,
began a solo ministry in 1979, with the recording of two albums of original songs for Benson's Impact Records, followed
by two more on Word's DaySpring label. Several more albums
have been released since then.

Jensen said of his personal appearances, "My goal in being
anywhere before people is to exalt the Lord Jesus Christ through
the gifts He has entrusted me with. Nothing of real value could
occur if I were there for any other purpose." In addition to "I
Should Have Been Crucified," among Jensen's songs are such

outstanding favorites as "He's as Close as the Mention of His Name," "Bigger than Any Mountain," "Tears Are a Language," "God Still Loves the World," and "Written in Red." His "Redemption Draweth Nigh" was used as the musical theme for the film *A Distant Thunder*.

In 1986, a nurse told Jensen of her participation in a late-term abortion in which a baby was born alive. When the infant began to cry, the nurse made an effort to help it but was told to "get away from that fetus and let it die." Jensen's response to her story was the writing of a song, "Sometimes They Cry." It received wide acceptance and was given a large amount of play on radio stations. He later said, "I'm hoping the Lord will use this song to stir some people to action."

Jensen has been nominated on five occasions for Songwriter of the Year by the Gospel Music Association, and a number of his songs have been listed among the Gospel Music Association's Top Ten Songs of the Year. His compositions are found in songbooks as well as in several choral collections.

In an interview in July 2001, I asked him to tell me how he came to write "I Should Have Been Crucified":

"In 1971, I read a biography of Billy Sunday in which a portion of one of his sermons appeared. In the sermon he used a graphic illustration, one that had a profound effect on me. It was the story of a man who should have died in the Civil War but his life was spared.

"During the struggle between the Union and the Confederate forces, a man from the South became a member of a Confederate group called Quantrell's Raiders. They used guerilla warfare tactics, raiding small towns and villages and then disappearing in the night. They were successful in avoiding being caught for a span of about two years.

"One night, the Union forces had been tipped off and were lying in wait for them. They were successful in capturing all of the Raiders but one, a teenage boy who escaped. The rest were sentenced to be executed before a firing squad. Word of the execution traveled over the countryside and a sizable crowd of spectators gathered to witness the fate of this notorious band. Little did the authorities know that the teen who had escaped made his way back to the scene and was present in the curious crowd.

"The raiders were lined up facing the firing squad. Just before the shots rang out, the young boy ran out of the crowd and up to the commanding officer. He yelled, 'Stop! I think you should know that I'm one of them. But you didn't bring me here; I came by my own choice.' He then pointed to one of the men in the line and said, 'This man is my friend. He has a wife and children, and I have no one. I'd like to take his place, if you will let him go.' The officer in charge replied, 'If that is your desire, I will grant it.' The teen walked into the line, in place of his friend, and was executed with Quantrell's Raiders.

"The freedman later became very successful in business and late in his life was a supporter of evangelist Billy Sunday. He also had a monument placed at the grave of the teen who died in his place. The inscription read:

> Sacred to the memory of Willie Lee.
> He took my place in the line.
> He died for me.

"My mind was set ablaze when I read this story in Billy Sunday's sermon. It illustrated 'Calvary' and all that it means to me. The whole thing came together in my mind one afternoon as I sat in the seats of the auditorium of Hammond High School in Hammond, Indiana, waiting for sound checks to be made in preparation for the evening's concert. I wrote the lyrics then and there, and in my mind I had a melody for it. The Orrells, a Southern Gospel group that I was singing with, were the first to record it. The Benson Company published it, and it was soon being recorded by many other groups."

"I Should Have Been Crucified" is one of approximately three hundred songs written by Gordon Jensen, many of which are favorites and have been heard and sung by millions of people worldwide.

Reflection

In his song, Gordon Jensen takes us in our sinful condition to the crucifixion scene and Christ's substitutionary death. One particular line, "Jesus, God's Son took my place," is deeply meaningful and, like the whole of the song, couched in the Scriptures. The Bible tells us that when Jesus went to the cross for you and me, He despised the shame (Heb. 12:2).

31

The Dream of a Totally Radical Guy

My Tribute

John 17:1–26

*And now, O Father, glorify thou me with thine
own self with the glory which I had with thee before
the world was.*

*A*ndrae Crouch has no doubt had the most varied musical career and ministry of any songwriter in America—from a choral arranger, conductor, and choirmaster on the children's animated film *Lion King*, to songwriter, singer, and pastor of the New Christ Memorial Church in Los Angeles. CeCe Winans, Christian soloist and part of the famed Winans family, said, "Andrae's music has had by far the most impact on my family and me, and that impact has probably grown over the years because his music is still the greatest."

There are many ways to honor the achievements of a great songwriter. The honors and awards that have come to Andrae Crouch are too numerous to list in this story, but the most sincere way to recognize and honor him is to sing his songs in a manner that is an earnest "tribute" to his Savior. Andrae has received to himself the blessings of his music many times over, as he heard others sing his compositions. As you will see in this story, he does not want the acclaim of his music to be tied to his own name or reputation. He truly wants the Lord to be glorified in it all.

Andrae's musical ability was a singular gift from God. He had no formal training on the piano prior to learning one Sunday morning in church that he could in fact play. It was a total surprise to him and his family. He has been playing the piano ever since.

There are perhaps thousands of stories that could be told as a result of someone hearing "My Tribute," but here I'd like to relate the story behind the song, which I consider to be Andrae's greatest. In an interview in 2001, he told me the following story:

"When I was eighteen, God called me to work in the Los Angeles Center of Teen Challenge, a recovery ministry for young people. The founder was David Wilkerson, author of the famed book *The Cross and the Switchblade*. A few of the people from Teen Challenge had visited our church during our radio broadcasts, so they knew me. I was the music guy at my dad's church, so I talked with Dad about the opportunity.

"I made the decision to work with Teen Challenge and went to a large house, much like a huge mansion. During my first day at the center, I saw this guy, Larry Reed, half white and half Mexican, who had been released from San Quentin Prison—an atheist who didn't want anything to do with the Lord. But he began to really love my music. He often would threaten to leave the center and I would take him into the chapel and play music for him. I would tell him, 'Man, don't leave. You've been paroled to this place. It will really mess things up for you if you leave.' I would persuade him to stay another night.

"Larry finally got saved and turned his life around. He turned out to be a radical guy—totally radical. If he walked into a room where everyone was talking quietly, he would yell, 'Praise the Lord! Hallelujah!' Everyone would always say, 'Well, here comes Larry.'

"Larry was always talking about what the Lord told him, or what he had read. We were happy to see his enthusiasm, compared to what he used to be, but he continued to be a loud guy! Often I would take a music group from the center to sing for other churches. Many times they were very conservative churches, and I would present our most subdued music. When Larry would make the trips with us, I sometimes called on him to give a testimony. He would get up and shout, 'Praise the Lord!' It would plaster people to the walls! I often wanted to say, 'Larry, could you hold it down a little?' But I would let it go by and laugh about it.

"Larry was at the center for two of the three-and-a-half to four years that I was there. At the end of my stay at Teen Challenge, I went back to my home church to continue my music ministry there. I wondered what God had done in my life during my time at the center. I was thanking God for those experiences when I received a phone call from Larry Reed. He had been gone from the center for more than a year.

"He said, 'Hey Andy!' I asked, 'Who is this?' And he said, 'This is Larry. *Praise God!*' I kind of chuckled. He said, 'I had a dream about you the other night.' I said, 'What is it now, Larry?' He was always having 'visions' or saying 'thus saith the Lord.' He said, 'I dreamed that you were going to write a song that is going to go around the world. It will be the biggest song you ever wrote, to this day.' I asked, 'Well, what do I have to read?' And he said, 'Read John, chapter 17, a passage about Jesus before He went back to heaven and His glory.' In that passage Jesus said, 'Father, I have glorified Thee, now glorify me.' I read the passage and didn't feel anything—no inspiration to write.

"The following morning, I got up singing 'to God be the glory.' I asked myself, 'Where did that come from?' I quickly got my tape recorder and taped the line I had just sung. I then went to the piano—I had a small apartment in the rear of my parents' home—and wrote 'My Tribute' in about ten minutes. I played it for my mother and she said, 'Praise the Lord.' I had forgotten that Larry had called, so I didn't connect my song with the Scriptures he had suggested I read.

"That evening, I was to visit in the home of my godchild, a

Filipino kid, where I was scheduled to have dinner. I played the song for them and we were all weeping around the piano. We sang 'My Tribute' for about an hour. I couldn't believe that the Lord had given me a song of that caliber. At that time I had only been writing songs for a relatively short period of time.

"We went to the table and began to eat and I said, 'Hey! Guess who called me yesterday?' They asked, 'Who?' I said, 'Larry Reed!' They chuckled—they knew Larry—and then I told them about Larry's prediction that I would write a song that would go all over the world. My friend Carrie Gonzalo said, 'You just wrote a song this morning.' I said, 'Yes, but it can't be that song.' She suggested that we read the Scripture that Larry had told me to read. We read the passage as we sat there. 'I have glorified thee on the earth: I have finished the work which thou gavest me to do. And now, O Father, glorify thou me with thine own self with the glory which I had with thee before the world was' (John 17:4–5). I gasped and said, 'It's all about *glory!*'

"A short time later, we recorded another album, *Keep on Singing,* and included 'My Tribute' in the project. I deliberately did not sing the solo part on that song. I had someone else sing it. I don't know why I was stubborn about that. I convinced myself that it was perhaps not the song that Larry had dreamed about.

"After the album had been out for a while, Ralph Carmichael, a songwriter, arranger, and conductor, said, 'Andrae, everyone is singing your song, "My Tribute." This is going to be your biggest song to date, and it will outlast you.' So later, on another album that we titled *Finally,* I recorded it, and *I* sang the solo part. There was such a span of time between those two albums that hundreds of people had already recorded it before I ever sang the solo part on a recording. I didn't want people to listen to the song solely because Andrae Crouch was singing it. I let a group who had not sung very much debut the song."

The rest is musical history. Since 1971, thousands of people have recorded "My Tribute" and millions have been blessed by hearing it. Having been translated into many languages, it has literally gone around the world, much as Larry Reed predicted. I could sense that Andrae was very pleased when he told me, "Larry Reed really loves God, and he preaches all over the country."

Reflection

The greatest spiritual goal that you and I can ever set is to glorify our heavenly Father with our lives. Let's make Jesus' life our example, and if there be any praise, "to God be the glory!"

32

The Extreme Love of a Sister

It's Still the Cross

1 Corinthians 1:10–25

For the preaching of the cross is to them that perish foolishness; but unto us which are saved it is the power of God.

$\mathcal{I}$ have often said that most of the songs that are very meaningful to Christians were written out of the sufferings and hardships of the children of God. Out of this dismay or darkness often comes a ray of sunshine, a song! I will be forever grateful that God has given to many of His servants the ability to "overcome" no matter what the circumstances.

Niles Borop III is a giant among songwriters, a man who for nearly half a century has lived in the shadow of ill health—yet, through the grace of God in his life, he has been able to rise above it and be enormously creative. While others have given us dozens, or perhaps a few hundred songs, Niles has written more than thirteen hundred, with nearly six hundred of those being recorded. His production in the realm of Christian music is unsurpassed by modern day songwriters.

He is the only nonperforming writer to have received two Dove Award nominations for Songwriter of the Year. He has three Dove Awards and has received numerous other Dove Award nominations. In 2003, his song "We Need to Thank God" won the *Singing News* Fan Award as the Favorite Song of the Year, as sung by the Inspirations.

Borop was born in Aiken, South Carolina, in 1956, the son of Dr. Niles Borop Jr. and his wife, Meta. They had their hands full when young Niles III was born with only one kidney, which itself was diseased. During the first year of his life, he underwent surgery more than twenty times. On three or four occasions during that year, the doctors gave him up for dead, and yet he survived. He had his last major surgery when he was four years old. After the operation, the doctor told his parents, "Take him home and enjoy him; I don't know how long you will have him."

Well, young Niles lived and became a very industrious teenager, giving his heart to Christ at age fourteen. It may sound strange, but two years before his conversion, he sensed that God wanted him to preach the gospel. During those early years, he began to study guitar and write songs. He wanted to communicate his biblical messages, so he sang at every opportunity.

After high school he went on to Mercer University, a Baptist school in Macon, Georgia, and graduated with honors after accomplishing a triple major—speech, dramatic arts, and education. Soon thereafter, he and Stephanie Lyle were married. He was accepted at a number of divinity schools but chose one primarily because it was in Nashville. Some years later, the time he spent at that school figured into the writing of "It's Still the Cross."

After receiving a master of divinity degree, he became a pastor, first at Dogwood Christian Church in Hopkinsville, Kentucky, for seven years, and then at Donaldson Christian Church in Nashville for eighteen months. Because they were small churches, and he was not a performing singer, they scarcely heard his music or knew he was a songwriter. He was assured in his own heart that his biblical calling was to be an evangelist, and he was sincerely grateful that God had given him the vehicle of music with which to get out a biblical message to many more thousands than he could ever reach with his speaking.

In 1987, after receiving numerous awards, honors, and plaques for his songwriting, and while at the top of his profession, he heard some alarming news. Niles told me, "I found out that I was losing my only kidney, and that I faced the prospect of death without a transplant. Quite frankly, all of the worldly successes became meaningless very quickly. I had no idea that my sisters could donate, or if they would. It was a breaking time for me. So, I packed up all of those awards and put them in a closet and left them there for five years. They were, at the time, my only feedback for my work, and they took on a value and a meaning for themselves that was not appropriate. It took me a long time to recognize that and to get over it. I needed to perceive that my worth and value is not based on what other people think but on what Christ has called me to do and whether or not I am obedient to Him." During that time, in 1991, Niles's sister Catherine donated one of her kidneys to him.

I asked Niles to tell me about the writing of "It's Still the Cross" and the following is what he told me:

"I am a graduate of Vanderbilt Divinity School, a very liberal place. Some were puzzled that I was able to get through that program, because most of what they teach is far from what I believe. But that course of study put a burning in my heart to communicate that we are not to lose sight of the foundation of our faith. It boils down to something very simple: it is still the blood and the sacrifice of Christ on the cross that redeems us and sets us free. It allows us to have an unfettered relationship with the heavenly Father. All of the philosophies and extreme teaching that are so prevalent do not really matter. We must not displace or elude the fact that it is the compassion and love of Christ, as He willingly gave Himself for us, that makes all the difference.

"'It's Still the Cross' was, in reality, written by several people—a group process. In 1994, Buddy Mullins had brought the basic concept and the seed thought to me at an earlier meeting. We had gotten together and exchanged our thoughts on the subject of the cross of Christ. I then met with Luke Garrett and Mike Harlen and shared with them what Buddy had brought to me and what our ideas were about this subject.

"I basically wrote the lyric, and Mike and Luke primarily wrote the musical setting. Of course, there was a lot of give-and-take between the three of us about both the lyric and the music. Sometimes it takes a long time to get a song just the way you think it ought to be, but in this case it all came together rather quickly. The passion that I felt about this subject had been brewing in me for years. The circumstances seemed to be right and I wrote it down as the Lord dictated it to me.

"I feel that Mike and Luke did a masterful job in musically interpreting what the Lord had given to me. The verses are very intense, while the chorus gives the bottom-line remedy for all problems of the heart. Although Mike and Luke changed places at the piano quite often that day, Luke was actually sitting at the piano during most of the writing."

May God continue to bring the message of this song to the ears and hearts of thousands who need to be reminded of the basic truths of the lyrics. Pray for Niles that God will give him many fruitful years of labor and that his songs will be all that the Lord intends for them to be.

Reflection

Though many men in history were crucified, only the crucifixion of the sinless Son of God was worthy to be the heavenly Father's eternal plan for mankind's salvation. The cross should be a constant reminder to each of us of the goodness of God in allowing His only Son to die in that manner and to die in our place.

33

The Triumph of a Sunday School Teacher
High and Lifted Up

John 12:23–33

*And I, if I be lifted up from the earth, will draw all
men unto me.*

From the age of twelve, Dianne Wilkinson has had an unbelievable rise in influence in the world of Southern Gospel Music. That genre of music has held her rapt attention since those early years. Through her lifespan as a wife, church pianist, faithful church member, Sunday school teacher, songwriter, and businesswoman, she has been a dedicated, loyal servant of Christ.

Dianne was born in Blytheville, Arkansas, in 1944, and while she was still a young child her mother, Blanche, and her Aunt Mavis introduced her to the world of Southern Gospel Music. They often would take her to the Ellis Auditorium in nearby Memphis, Tennessee, to hear such famed groups of that era as the Blackwood Brothers, the Statesmen, the Speer Family, and the LeFevres, just to name a few.

When Dianne was eight, her grandmother strongly suggested that she start taking piano lessons. She did so and progressed so rapidly that she was soon playing the piano for church

143

services. At age twelve, she began singing with her mother and her aunt in a trio they called the Ross Sisters. She also was the pianist for the group. They sang in numerous churches in and around their hometown and on a number of radio programs.

Dianne Wilkinson has a great love for her Southern heritage, her Southern Gospel Music, and her Southern Baptist church. For a number of years she has been the pianist at Springhill Baptist Church in Dyersburg, Tennessee, where her brother, James Branscum, is the pastor. She also teaches the Open Door Sunday School Class. The church members certainly know of her fame as a songwriter, but they love her mostly for her faithful service to her church family. She told me, "I have always had a music ministry in my church, and that is my calling."

When Dianne was in her early twenties, the Lord led her into serious study of the Word of God. With her Bible, commentaries, and other study materials, she equipped herself as a teacher and a songwriter. This preparation resulted in the writing of songs that were true to the Word of God, and quality teaching for the Open Door class.

Over the following twenty years, Dianne wrote almost three hundred songs. Some of them have become standards—songs such as "We Shall See Jesus," which became the signature song of Glenn Payne of the Cathedrals, and "Boundless Love," seemingly a favorite of all who hear it. Sixteen of her songs were recorded by the Cathedrals alone. Many others have put her songs on their albums. Dianne said, "When you are writing for the Cathedrals and you love quartet music like I do, so much of it comes out straight ahead, quartet to the bone. And that is really what I'm doing these days. Traditional quartets are more popular than ever, and they're always looking for new songs that sound old."

One day, Dianne heard a sermon about the brazen serpent being lifted up by Moses in the wilderness, and how all who looked on it were healed of the fiery serpent bites. The preacher also reminded his hearers of the passage in John 3 where Jesus said, "And as Moses lifted up the serpent in the wilderness, even so must the Son of man be lifted up."

Following is how Dianne finished her story: "I began to think about the Cross, and how Christ was lifted up, giving His life for each of us that we might be saved. I also began to think of how He would be lifted up a second time, not on a cross but in all of His glory. As I began to write, I wanted to contrast the two, and so I began to paint word pictures. After I developed the two scenes in my mind, it didn't take long to put it on paper.

"I showed the song to Roger Bennett, the pianist for the Cathedrals, and he graciously informed me that it still needed some work. Roger felt that the melody I had written for the chorus would be difficult to harmonize. I was hesitant at first, because I usually didn't rewrite after I had finished a song. But I prayed about it and thought, 'Lord, maybe we do need to put a tweak here and there.' I only slightly changed the first line or two of the chorus.

"The Cathedrals made the decision to record it. In fact, they chose my song 'High and Lifted Up' as the title song for their project. Lari Goss, who had done all of the orchestration and produced the complete work, was present in the studio during the recording. It was a class act from beginning to end. They also included another of my songs on the project, 'Jesus Has Risen.' The following year, it received the *Singing News* Fan Award as Song of the Year."

Dianne Wilkinson has often been told by her friends that "High and Lifted Up" is her best song. In it she takes the biblical message concerning Christ's death and makes it live again in the hearts of believers, while giving a message of salvation to the lost as she tells of "reconciling God and man forever." Then, in the chorus, with her majestic melody and lyric, she lets us see Christ "high and lifted up in all His glory."

This song has crossed over from the Southern Gospel genre

of music to many of the more traditional church music programs, especially with the masterful choral arrangement by Tom Fettke. What a thrill to hear a large church choir and orchestra as they become totally engrossed in the power of this great musical offering.

Dianne continues to write songs and minister in her church. She also writes a column for *U.S. Gospel News,* a Southern Gospel Music magazine, and has spoken in seminars for songwriters, encouraging them and passing on some of her experiences as a composer.

Reflection

God has commanded us in Colossians 3:16 to teach and admonish one another with psalms and hymns and spiritual songs, and at the same time to sing with grace in our hearts to the Lord. "High and Lifted Up" certainly helps us to do just that.

34

They Didn't Want the Gory Songs

I Will Glory in the Cross

Galatians 6:1–15

But God forbid that I should glory, save in the cross of our Lord Jesus Christ, by whom the world is crucified unto me, and I unto the world.

*D*ottie Rambo excels as a woman who has greatly influenced the world of Southern Gospel Music. It all started in the rural town of Madisonville, Kentucky, when she was only eight years old. She came home one day and began to quote a poem to her mother, who was cooking in the kitchen. Dottie had just come from the creek bank where she had composed the verses.

He mother began to weep with joy as she realized that her little girl, one of her eleven children, had a wonderful gift from the Lord. By age eleven, Dottie had begun to write songs, one of which was sung by the Happy Goodman Family and recorded by Jimmy Davis, then governor of Louisiana.

As the years went by, God gave Dottie hundreds of songs, many of which are sung by people around the world and have been recorded by thousands of artists. Scattered among those triumphs were periods of heartache and disappointment. Yet out of these dark days came some of her most blessed songs. During an interview, she told me that she and her family went through some rough times in the mid-1970s. She related the following story to me:

"We were doing a lot of concerts, competitive concerts, making a lot of money. Suddenly I realized that I was not living close to the Lord. I was not writing under the anointing of the Holy Spirit. I also realized that I had never done anything to merit all of this goodness, recognition, and fame.

"I then began to study the Scriptures where Paul said that he didn't glory in himself (Galatians 6:14). I came back to the realization that all I have is because of the grace of God and the Cross of Christ.

"During this time we went to Holland to do a number of concerts. When we got off the plane, people met us and took us to a little quaint hotel. As we rode along, they informed us that while we were there singing in the concerts, we were not to sing about the Cross of Christ. I looked at the young man who was escorting us and asked, 'Do you mean that we are not allowed to sing about the Cross to these Christians?' He said, 'No, they consider it gory. They don't want to hear about the blood or the Cross.' I then looked at him (I was old enough to be his mother) and said, 'Son, if you won't tell them you told me this, then I will pretend I don't know it. Because, I *will* be singing about the Cross and about the blood of Christ.'

"We sang in the concert that very night, 'He Looked Beyond My Fault and Saw My Need.' People were weeping all over the audience, even the man who sent the message that we were not to sing about the Cross of Christ. The Lord really seemed to move in the hearts of the people.

"We went back to the little hotel that evening and to bed. I lay there in the darkness and began to weep. I said, 'God, I apologize that we wouldn't want to hear about the blood of Christ, His Cross, and His grace. I really apologize.' As I lay there, the Lord began to give me a song. I kept it all in my heart until the next morning when I awoke to write it down."

The song that she wrote as she lay there in the darkened room has a thought not expressed in any other musical composition that I have ever heard. "I will weep no more for the cross that He bore, but I will glory in the cross."

What an amazing story and what a glorious song! Dottie realized, as you and I should, that the gift of God for a lost world is something for which to thank Him, something for which to give Him glory and praise.

In the song she puts everything in the right perspective as she recalls her feeling while studying Galatians 6. So, she began her song. "I boast not of works, or tell of good deeds." We have nothing that would gain for us a place at the "table of Life." Only His love will make provision for us to partake.

Dottie Rambo, following great periods of sickness and surgeries, continues to travel across our nation, singing her songs and blessing the hearts of Christians. She told me, "I asked the Lord to let me, at least once each year, write a song that will speak to the hearts of Christians everywhere." Her songs might not have come with that frequency, but in the Lord's time He gave to all of us, through Dottie, so many wonderful musical treasures.

Reflection

I, too, have nothing in which to glory, save in the blessed truth of the death, burial, and resurrection of our blessed Lord. By His marvelous grace He included you—and me—in His kindness.

35

They Ruined My Song

I'm Feeling Fine

John 14:1–15

In my Father's house are many mansions: if it were not so, I would have told you. I go to prepare a place for you.

$\mathcal{M}$osie Lister has had a varied musical career as a singer, songwriter, and vocal arranger. All three of those gifts from the Lord were evident very early in his life. Today, at age eighty-one, songs and choral arrangements continue to flow from his creative, youthful mind. He freely calls the songs gifts from God. Very few songwriters have been as prolific and have had as many extremely popular songs flow from their pens.

These days, Mosie not only continues to write songs, but he is also an effective choral arranger, primarily associated with Lillenas, a music production company that is a subsidiary of the Nazarene Publishing House. After his company, Mosie Lister Publications, merged with Lillenas in 1969, he was able to give his time fully to writing and arranging. Mosie has always said, "I want to write music that moves the heart and stirs the soul."

The popularity of his songs is evident in the fact that thousands of Southern Gospel Music singers have recorded them, as well as a sizable number of popular singers such as Elvis

Presley, Jimmy Dean, George Beverly Shea, Loretta Lynn, Merle Haggard, B. J. Thomas, and Floyd Cramer, just to name a few.

The following account is the story behind one of the classics from Lister's pen, just as he told it:

"I used to listen to a particular group on the radio in Atlanta that had a tenor singer who liked to sing slow songs and get to the top of his range and just croon, with voices backing him up. I thought, 'I would love to write a song in that style.'

"I wrote a song, imagining what that particular high tenor would sound like if he were singing my song. The whole of it was built around the idea, 'I'm feeling fine, because I've got heaven on my mind.' I really don't know where the original thought came from.

"A few days passed, and I showed it to no one. I received a call from Urias LeFevre of the LeFevre Trio. He asked if I had any new songs. I said, 'Yes,' and I took my new song to their home. They quickly began working on it. They even recorded it, and I didn't even know it. A month or so later, I heard it being sung on the radio.

"I was surprised when I heard my song being sung in a fast tempo—really fast. My response was one of shock. I thought they had completely ruined my song. But they sounded as if they were enjoying it, and it moved along quite well. They started including it during personal appearances. Other groups began to sing it.

"The Blackwood Brothers went to New York City to sing on the *Arthur Godfrey Show,* and they carried my song and used it during the week that they were there. From there the song began to spread. It went from one place to another. People enjoy singing 'I'm Feeling Fine' because it is *fun* to sing.

"Thanks, Eva Mae LeFevre. If you hadn't taken my slow song and sung it fast, I don't think anyone else would have ever listened to it."

Mosie Lister has recently written a sequel to his song, which he titled "I'm Still Feeling Fine." It is high on the *Singing Music* and *U.S. Gospel News* charts.

Reflection

Wouldn't it be tremendous if we, in our Christian journey, came often to the point of "feeling fine," prompted by thoughts of spending eternity with our heavenly Father, who loves us and gave His Son to provide a way for us to come unto Himself?

36

Trying on Thomas's Shoes

Jesus, Lord to Me

John 20:19–31

And Thomas answered and said unto him,
My Lord and my God.

*T*wo of the most prominent names in Christian music, Gary McSpadden and Greg Nelson, combined their talents to give us one of the great songs of Christian dedication. Though the two are from backgrounds that are extremely different, the Lord brought them together and used their individual, dedicated, and unique abilities to craft a song that has been a blessing to untold multitudes of Christians—a song born right out of the Scriptures.

Gary McSpadden was born into the home of a preacher in Mangum, Oklahoma, in 1943. His parents, Boyd and Helen McSpadden, later moved to Lubbock, Texas, where Reverend Boyd became pastor of Faith Temple. Gary grew up in an extremely musical home. His mother and father were both songwriters, and at least one of their compositions, "Heaven," became quite popular after George Beverly Shea and a number of others recorded it.

Gary was like many preacher's kids who have grown up in church. He took his salvation for granted. But "on my fourteenth birthday," he said, "I gave my heart completely to Christ.

I made an exchange with God. I gave Him nothing and He gave me everything."

In addition to singing with his sister, Cheryl, now a talented vocalist and the wife of Dino Kartsonakis, he sang as a soloist in the church from the age of ten. His voice began to mature and improve to the point that he was brought to the attention of Hovie Lister, manager of the Statesmen quartet. When Gary was eighteen, he was invited to sing with the Statesmen for a period of about five months while Jake Hess was on a medical leave.

After his short stint with the Statesmen, he joined the Oak Ridge Boys for a while. In 1964, he was instrumental in the starting of the Imperials, and he sang with them for just under four years. From there he went back to working with his father, who by then was the pastor of the Christian Center in Fort Worth, Texas. Gary completely stopped touring and worked at the church for ten years. Following this period when he did not sing professionally, he joined the Bill Gaither Trio and sang with Bill and Gloria Gaither and with the Gaither Vocal Band for eleven years.

A brief account of Greg Nelson's early life is shared elsewhere in this volume in the story behind the song "We Are So Blessed." You'll be encouraged as Gary tells how "Jesus, Lord to Me" was written:

"I was reading the Bible one day and was thinking of Thomas in terms of his doubting. We all have our 'Thomas' moments. I tried to put myself in Thomas's shoes and asked myself, 'What would I have thought if I had watched Jesus die, and later they had come to me and told me, "He's alive!"' I might have concluded, 'These people are nuts,' depending on my level of belief. Then, in my imagination I could hear Thomas say, after placing his hands in the wounds of Jesus, 'Now I know You, and now I see that You are Lord of all, and You are Lord to me.'

"Even though we might have an occasional 'Thomas' moment, we must personally get to the place where we believe in Christ's death, burial, and resurrection, with all of our hearts. Then we can sing with sincerity, *Jesus, Lord to me.*

"I completed the writing of the lyrics and had a portion of a melody when I decided that I wanted someone of the talent and stature of Greg Nelson to have a part in this project with me. I invited Greg to my home, shared the lyrics with him, and we talked briefly about the idea I had concerning a melody. Nothing further was done with the song at my home that day. Greg took the lyrics and the ideas that I shared with him and later wrote the musical setting, just as you see it in print today.

"Afterward, while I was on a cruise, I had an opportunity to show the new song to Sandi Patti, who liked it and agreed to record it. That helped to launch it on its way around the world. Many others have recorded 'Jesus, Lord to Me,' and it now appears in hymnals and has been translated into other languages."

Gary and his wife, Carol, have two married children and several grandchildren. They now make their home in Branson, Missouri, where Gary continues his songwriting, music publishing, and promotion of Southern Gospel concerts. He produces and appears on a weekly television program that is seen internationally. Gary often speaks in seminars or for church services on a variety of subjects. Tyndale House Publishers released a series of recordings, *Drive Time Devotions*, on which Gary presents twenty devotional stories—three to four minutes each—including Scriptures, a prayer, and a challenge. He is an inductee into the Gospel Music Association Hall of Fame.

Reflection

Making Jesus the Master and Lord of our lives is the most important part of our existence. Someone has said, "Christ will either be Lord *of* all, or He will not be Lord *at* all."

37

Unexpectedly and Wonderfully Blessed

Surely the Presence of the Lord Is in This Place

Psalm 16:1–11

Thou wilt show me the path of life: in thy presence is fulness of joy; at thy right hand there are pleasures for evermore.

Extraordinary is one word that describes Lanny Wolfe's life and labors. In addition to his songwriting, his educational pursuits are stellar. He earned two bachelor's degrees, two master's degrees, and was granted an honorary doctorate. He was dean of the School of Music in three different colleges and was founder of the National Music Ministry Conference in Jackson, Mississippi. Lanny Wolfe has also had a most colorful career as a singer and songwriter.

Born in Columbus, Ohio, to Pearl and Precious Wolfe, Lanny was exposed to music early on—his mother sang and played guitar at many revivals and special church services. Lanny, his brother, Larry, and his sister, Sharon, rode the city bus to church as children. Lanny said of his salvation experience at age eleven, "I gave my heart to the Lord, was baptized, and received His Spirit."

Lanny gives others credit for his early music training and experience. "Two people helped nurture my love for music in general, and gospel music in particular—Ruth Morgan, my junior high school teacher, and Lois Newstrand, a pastor's wife who played piano and organ, directed choirs, and who allowed a teenager to play piano for the camp choir."

In more than four decades of interviews, I have had many songwriters relate to me that the Lord suddenly dropped a song into their hearts. Some even said that they were not expecting to write a song, that the experience came as a complete surprise. But what happened to Lanny one day in Columbus, Mississippi, is different from all the rest. In 1977, he had gone there with the Lanny Wolfe Trio to participate in a very important church function. He relates his experience:

"We were there to be a part of the festivities for the dedication of a new church auditorium. The mayor of the city was there, along with a number of other dignitaries and officials. The newness of the building was apparent, and everyone was dressed properly and in his or her place. It was everything you might expect at a church dedication.

"While other festivities were taking place and our trio was waiting to sing, the Lord suddenly dropped a tune and a lyric right into my head. What was unusual about this incident was that the music went in a certain progression that I would not ordinarily go to, especially not being at a keyboard. But, as I sat there, the Lord gave me the whole chorus.

"When it was time for us to sing, I stepped to the piano and began singing the new song, just as the Lord had given it to me. When I finished singing it through one time, I then taught it to the audience. The other members of our group were learning it along with the congregation."

Lanny's musical message reminded the people gathered there that the Lord was present with them as they were assembled in His name. They could sense God's "mighty power and His grace." As Lanny observed others around him, he sang that he could see the glory of the Lord "on each face," an indication that the "presence of the Lord" had come into their church that day.

In the foyer of that Columbus church hangs a framed scrap of paper on which Lanny scribbled the words to his song while still seated at the piano, and as the Lord was giving it. It is a reminder to the congregation of what happened in their midst on that special day—a memento that they witnessed the birth of a famous song. "Surely the Presence of the Lord Is in This Place" has never been changed and has gone around the world.

The honors that have come to Lanny Wolfe as a result of his talented songwriting are numerous. He was SESAC's Gospel Composer of the Year in 1975 and 1976. He won a Dove Award as the Gospel Music Association's Songwriter of the Year in 1984, for his song "More Than Wonderful," which was voted Song of the Year. Other awards too numerous to mention here have come to Lanny. There will probably be other times of recognition in the future as he continues to write songs and musicals that bless the church of God.

Lanny now resides in Houston, Texas, where he oversees the ministry of his company, Paragon Music Productions. He also travels to many places in our nation conducting his successful choir clinics. Let me have Lanny close this story for you:

"What does God have in store for Lanny Wolfe? I don't really know, but I've learned that whatever God wants to do, He will do it in spite of anything or anybody—and that includes Lanny Wolfe. As for now, I'm gonna trust Him, I'm gonna trust Him, I'm gonna trust Him all my life."

Reflection

When you and I feel the presence of the Lord in our lives, it is His goodness that allows such a thing, and it is wonderful! Remember, the Bible says, "In thy presence is fulness of joy" (Psalm 16:11).

38

What Song Are You Whistling?

Holy Spirit, Thou Art Welcome

John 16:7–15

Nevertheless I tell you the truth; It is expedient for
you that I go away: for if I go not away, the
Comforter will not come unto you; but if I depart, I
will send him unto you.

$\mathcal{I}$f you would like to meet Andy Griffith in person, raise your hand! I daresay most every person reading this book has his hand up right now. How would you like to have worked alongside him on one of his projects? Well, David Huntsinger has done so. He arranged the music for Andy Griffith's 1995 CD, *Precious Memories*—possibly the most successful hymn CD in history and still going! David had the pleasure of being invited to Andy's home in North Carolina to talk about the project before they began to work on it. David was still excited about it when I talked with him on November 20, 2003.

David Huntsinger was born in Indianapolis in 1955. When he was only ten days old, his parents moved to Los Angeles, where he grew up. When he was eleven, his parents bought a piano from their family doctor for sixty-five dollars. David said, "I had never known I was interested in music at all, but with the coming of the piano, suddenly the interest was there. I was in love with it! I played constantly. I had a good ear for music and within a year I was playing for church services." He played piano and organ at the church until he graduated from high school.

David gave his heart and life to Christ in an Assembly of God church in Norwalk, California. He grew up in a congregation where music was extremely important. In the church, he had a combination of musical influences ranging from the more traditional music of Ralph Carmichael and Audrey Mieir to Southern Gospel. One day his mother bought a very early recording of the Rambos and David played it constantly. He said, "As a kid I liked their music."

He attended California State University, Long Beach, for two years, studying anthropology. Then he was approached by Hal Spencer, founder of Manna Music, about playing piano for the Rambos—Dottie, Buck, and Reba. He had been playing for a group called the Monarchs. He was recommended to Spencer by Andrae Crouch, who had seen David playing piano on television. Crouch said, "I've seen this kid on TV, and I don't know his name, but he's really good." Spencer located David and helped make the necessary contacts, and he was soon playing for the Rambos. He continued with them for three years.

David had written some songs earlier with his wife, Bonnie, whom he met as a young teenager—although they didn't date until after they graduated from high school. They were married in 1981. While with the Rambos, David became more serious about the song creation process. He says, "I loved observing the songwriting of Dottie Rambo." He worked with Reba (Rambo) McGuire on a record project called *Lady,* which contained a number of her songs. It was a number one album for an extended time.

While David was with the Rambos, Dottie knew that he was interested in songwriting, so together they wrote a very popular children's musical, "Down by the Creekbank." It was ironic, because Dottie's songwriting started by a creek bank when she was a small child. You can learn more of her early life in the stories of her songs that appear in this volume.

During David Huntsinger's tenure with the Rambos, Dottie would often watch the television ministry of Rex Humbard in Akron, Ohio. She noticed that Reverend Humbard would open his program with the statement, "Holy Spirit Thou art welcome in this place." She remarked to David, "That would be a good title for a song. Let's write one."

David told me, "I remember that we sat down on their bus and Dottie wrote the lyrics very quickly. I then began to work on the music. I said to her, 'I think it would be good to have a verse.' I had already been thinking of a melody. Dottie then wrote an additional lyric. It all happened, initially, in an hour or two at the most. On the Rambos' next record, they included 'Holy Spirit, Thou Art Welcome.' We also began to use it in the concerts. It took off very quickly. It was published in sheet music and in a choral arrangement and began to be sung very widely in churches.

"Not long after the song was written, I went to Canada to play for a concert. While at the airport picking up my luggage, I heard a gentleman nearby whistling a tune. I listened long enough to be sure that he was whistling the tune that I thought he was. I then broke into his music and engaged him in a bit of conversation. I asked, 'Sir, I am interested to know the name of the song you were whistling.' He said, '"Holy Spirit, Thou Art Welcome." We sing it at our church.' I said, 'I wrote that song with Dottie Rambo.' He looked at me like, 'No way!' That was the first time I had heard anyone, outside our concerts, sing—or whistle—the song after we wrote it. That experience I will never forget. The song has now gone around the world."

David and Bonnie, and their two dogs and two cats, live in the Nashville area where he continues to write, produce, and arrange music. David has done many records and CDs of his piano music, with orchestra, which have been well received. He has recently worked on a number of records for Discovery House Music, an arm of Radio Bible Class.

Reflection

I love "Holy Spirit, Thou Art Welcome" because it addresses the blessed third person of the Trinity, the heavenly Guest, who has taken up His abode in the hearts of those who know Christ as Lord and Savior. He is our Comforter, our Guide, and our Teacher.

39

Would Another Direction Be Better?

His Grace Is Sufficient for Me

2 Corinthians 12:1–10

And he said unto me, My grace is sufficient for thee: for my strength is made perfect in weakness.

$\mathcal{M}$osie Lister once said, "I sweat blood over most of the songs I write. I work hard at making them what I think they ought to be." Yet Mosie admits that there are rare exceptions when the songs almost seem to write themselves. They come very quickly and seldom need a lot of changing or editing. Some of his songs that have become enormously popular were written in as short a span as ten minutes.

Mosie's songs have been acclaimed by thousands of singers, simply by the fact that they have recorded them—singers such as the Statesmen Quartet, Gold City, the Inspirations, Elvis Presley, Loretta Lynn, and George Beverly Shea, just to name a few.

He has been complimented by other great songwriters such as Albert Brumley, who said, "'How Long Has It Been' (Lister's most popular song) is the greatest gospel song." When Brumley was asked, "How about your song 'I'll Fly Away'?" Mr. Brumley replied, "It's not in the same class."

I first met Mosie Lister in 1958, in Tampa, Florida. I had the privilege of visiting him in his home and of talking with him about his songwriting and his extensive music ministry. From subsequent interviews and from material published by Lillenas Publishing Company, which publishes Mosie's choral arrangements, musicals, and song collections, I am able to bring you this story. I hope you are inspired by the following, just as Mosie told it:

"'His Grace Is Sufficient for Me' was literally a gift from God. In the mid-1960s, I realized I had gone for an incredibly long time without writing a song that had real worth—that really meant something. It had been more than a year, and that was really rare for me. Though I sometimes worked on songs for several months, I never thought they were difficult to write. I had never been through a dry spell like that before. I began to search my mind and my heart.

"We were living in Tampa, Florida, then, and one morning I was driving downtown to pick up my mail. On the way I started thinking about how long it had been since I had written a song, and I just sincerely and honestly prayed to God about it. I told Him that I felt that I might be at a place in my life where He was pointing me in another direction—away from writing music. Yet I really loved it and felt that it was given to me from Him.

"I told God that I was despondent over not writing anything in a long time, and that I just didn't understand the reasons for it. I said, 'Right now I just give You whatever ability I have. If You want me to go in another direction and leave writing, I'll do that, and I will be happy about it. I just need to know what Your will is. If You'll show me Your will, I'll do it.'

"After returning home, I did what I had done very often in those days. I took my guitar, sat down, and starting strumming and humming to myself. I found myself singing, 'Many times I'm tried and tested as I travel day by day. . . .' I was on the second verse before it dawned on me what I was doing. It occurred to me that this was a new song, and I hadn't written one in over a year.

"I then thought of the verse in Scripture where Paul says, 'My grace is sufficient for thee' (2 Corinthians 12:9). That became the chorus of my song. Since then, I've never doubted that I'm doing exactly what God wants me to do. I feel that this song came along when I needed its message for my own heart."

Reflection

Sometimes, God seems to allow us to get to a point in our lives when we look up to Him in despair, thus giving Him the opportunity to assure us that His grace is truly sufficient for every trial or temptation.

Part 2

A Special Section of Classic Hymns and Gospel Songs Often Recorded and Performed by Southern Gospel Groups

40

A Church Mouse Moved the Play

Silent Night! Holy Night!

Luke 2:1–12

For unto you is born this day in the city of David a Saviour, which is Christ the Lord.

Thousands of Southern Gospel singing groups have recorded Christmas albums, cassettes, or CDs. Very few would omit the subject of this unusual story. The uniqueness that makes the song so attractive to the singing groups is the same characteristic that makes it a favorite in all the world. It would be almost impossible to live through a Christmas season on our planet without hearing the strains of this Austrian-born carol.

In 1818, a band of roving actors was performing throughout the little towns and hamlets of the Austrian Alps. One night the players came to the tiny village of Oberndorf, near Salzburg, for their annual presentation of the Christmas story.

The play was scheduled for St. Nicholas Church, but the organ bellows had been damaged by a mouse that ate a hole in the bellows, and they could not be repaired in time. The show was presented in a private home instead, and the church's assistant pastor, Joseph Mohr, attended.

As Mohr walked home that night through the new-fallen snow, his path led him over a small hill. Looking down on the little village below, Mohr was deeply impressed by the beauty of the glowing scene and the majestic silence of the wintry night. His thoughts took him back to the first Christmas—when angels spoke to faithful shepherds on a holy night such as this—and a poem began to form in his mind. He would later title it "Stille Nacht! Heilige Nacht!"

Arriving home, the pastor quickly penned the words that would inscribe his poem into history. He sincerely wished his poem could be sung at the church's upcoming Christmas service, but he had no music. The next day, Mohr rushed to the home of his good friend Franz Gruber, the church organist. It is reported that Gruber composed a musical setting the same day he received the poem.

On Christmas Day, Gruber and Mohr sang their new song to the congregation gathered in the little church. Because the organ was still in ill repair, Gruber accompanied them on his guitar, and "Silent Night! Holy Night!" was first introduced.

A few weeks later, an organ repairman arrived at the church to repair the damage done by the church mouse. As soon as the man finished his work, Gruber sat down to test the instrument. It is reported that the first song he played was his new Christmas composition. Deeply touched by the music, the repairman took a copy of the song back to his own Alpine village. There, a family of gifted Austrian singers, the Strasser Sisters, picked it up and began singing it throughout the countryside.

The Strasser quartet created a sensation, and the carol quickly became a European favorite. It was translated into English in 1863, by Jane Campbell, and made its first appearance in America in 1871 in Charles Hutchins's *Sunday School Hymnal.*

"Silent Night! Holy Night!" is as fresh and beautiful today as when it was first heard in the little Austrian town more than 170 years ago. Year after year we lovingly sing this simple tribute to our Savior, Jesus Christ.

> Silent night! holy night! All is calm all is bright,
> 'Round yon virgin mother and Child!

Holy Infant, so tender and mild,
Sleep in heavenly peace, sleep in heavenly peace.

Silent night! holy night! Shepherds quake at the sight,
Glories stream from heaven afar,
Heavenly hosts sing alleluia;
Christ the Savior is born! Christ the Savior is born!

Silent night! holy night! Son of God, love's pure light,
Radiant beams from Thy holy face,
With the dawn of redeeming grace,
Jesus, Lord at Thy birth! Jesus, Lord at Thy birth!

Pause for a few moments and reflect on the awesome fact that Jesus came to earth for you and me . . . to give us His peace. During the holiday season, we think of Him as a Babe in a manger—but He really came to this earth to die on a cross for the sins of the whole world, including your sins and mine—giving us "heavenly peace."

Reflection

God truly does bring peace into the hearts of every person who comes to Him in a personal way. *Peace* overflows our hearts when we realize that we are His children and that we are on our way to heaven to be with Him.

41

A Great Capacity for Love

My Savior First of All

John 20:26–31

*Reach hither thy finger, and behold my hands; and
reach hither thy hand, and thrust it into my side:
and be not faithless, but believing.*

In 1820, in Putnam County, New York, a doctor with a lack
of proper medical knowledge applied a mustard plaster poultice to the eyes of Frances Jane Crosby when she was only six
weeks old. It robbed her of her sight. Nevertheless, she grew to
be a cheerful, happy soul with a marvelous attitude. She accepted her handicap with an unusual reservoir of courage.

When she was only sixteen, she wrote, "His purposes will
ripen fast, unfolding every hour. The bud may have a bitter
taste, but sweet will be the flower." What a marvelous philosophy for one to have, especially a sixteen-year-old. But, add blindness to the equation and it adds up to an unusual young lady.

Fanny Crosby, as she was affectionately called, penned more
than eighty thousand songs in her lifetime, which spanned nearly
a century. She died in her ninety-fifth year, still a contented,
joyful soul. She had become one of the most notable names in
hymnody. Not even the loss of her eyesight could render defeat
to this courageous soul. S. Trevena Jackson, her biographer
and longtime friend, described her as a lady of diligent indus-

try, sincere unselfishness, unfailing joyousness, with a wonderful memory and a great capacity for sympathy.

Late in her life, Fanny related to Jackson some very personal experiences—scenes from her years as a young woman. They appear in Jackson's book, *Fanny Crosby's Story of Ninety-Four Years,* published by Fleming H. Revell Company in 1915. Before getting into the story behind the song for this chapter, I want to share Fanny's account of those events:

> Some people seem to forget that blind girls have just as great a faculty for loving, and do love just as much and just as truly as those who have their sight. When I was about twenty, a gifted young man by the name of Alexander Van Alstyne came to our Institute. He was also blind and very fond of classic literature and theological lore, but made music a specialty. After hearing several of my poems, he became deeply interested in my work; and I, after listening to his sweet strains of music, became interested in him. Thus we soon became very much concerned for each other. . . . I placed my right hand on his left and called him "Van." Then it was that two happy lovers sat in silence while the sunbeams danced around their heads, and the golden curtains of day drew in their light. Van took up the harp of love, and drawing his fingers over the golden chords, sang to me the song of a true lover's heart. From that hour two lives looked on a new universe, for love met love, and all the world was changed.
>
> We were no longer blind, for the light of love showed us where the lilies bloomed, and where the crystal waters find the moss-mantled spring. On March the fifth in the year 1858 we were united in marriage.
>
> Now I am going to tell you something that only my closest friends know. I became a mother and knew a mother's love. God gave us a tender baby, but the angels

came down and took our infant up to God and His throne. Van went home to his Father's house in the year 1902.[1]

The Chautauqua Institute, on Lake Chautauqua in western New York state, was a beloved place to Fanny Crosby. In the latter part of her life, she loved to spend at least a week there during their Bible conference. She often took part in the programs. It was also a week when she could fellowship with some of the most talented and influential Christian musicians of that era.

One evening, following one of the inspiring services, Aunt Fanny, as she was affectionately called, was sitting on the porch of the hotel chatting with John Sweney, a musician who had written the musical setting for a number of great hymns. They were discussing how wonderful it was to be able to come to such a place, away from the cares of the world, and enjoy the things of the Lord. They thought that it was just about the nearest thing to heaven a person could ask for.

"Fanny, speaking of heaven—I mean the real one that the Lord is preparing for His children—do you think we'll recognize each other?" asked Sweney. She replied, "John, I think we will. In fact, I agree with Annie Herbert who wrote, 'We shall know each better when the mists have rolled away.' But John, the question that is really on your mind is, 'Fanny, you're blind and you have never seen a human being before; therefore, how will you recognize your friends and especially the Lord?' To which I reply, John Sweney, I've thought about that quite often and I know that I will not have a bit of trouble recognizing my friends or my beautiful Savior; however, contemplating that there might be a problem, I have this to offer. Mind you, I still believe I won't have any problem; but just in case I do, I'll go to the one whom I feel is my Savior and will say, 'May I please look at Your hands?' John, I'll know it is my Savior by the print of the nails in His hands."

Sweney just didn't know how to respond for a few seconds. He then asked her if she could write some verses with those thoughts in mind. She promised that she would pray about it and then dismissed herself and went to bed. It was already past her bedtime. She told Sweney she would see him the next morning.

Early the next morning she called for John Sweney, who came to her room. She shared with him a poem that she had written:

> When my life work is ended, and I cross the swelling tide,
> When the bright and glorious morning I shall see,
> I shall know my Redeemer when I reach the other side,
> And His smile will be the first to welcome me.
>
> Chorus:
> I shall know Him, I shall know Him,
> And redeemed by His side I shall stand,
> I shall know Him, I shall know Him,
> By the print of the nails in His hand.
>
> Through the gates of the city in a robe of spotless white,
> He will lead me where no tears will ever fall;
> In the glad song of ages I shall mingle with delight,
> But I long to see my Savior first of all.

The musical setting for her lyrics was written by Sweney, who composed the music for two other great Crosby songs, "Take the World, but Give Me Jesus" and "Tell Me the Story of Jesus." "My Savior First of All" has long been a favorite for Southern Gospel singers and their audiences.

Reflection

When God allowed His only Son to be pierced in His hands and His side for you and me, it was an expression of love and a sacrifice for our sins that we will only fully understand when we see Him in heaven.

175

42

A Hit from the Start

The Battle Hymn of the Republic

1 Corinthians 15:12–25

*Christ the firstfruits; afterward they that are
Christ's at his coming. Then cometh the end, when
he shall have delivered up the kingdom to God,
even the Father; when he shall have put down all
rule and all authority and power. For he must
reign, till he hath put all enemies under his feet.*

*V*ery seldom do the people of the world pick a sacred song,
done in a simple yet beautiful way, and make it a "hit." But such
has been the case with Julia Ward Howe's "The Battle Hymn of
the Republic." It is uniquely spirited and lends itself to being
sung by a group of men. It is a marvelous song for many Southern Gospel quartets, especially during the season surrounding
Independence Day.

This song, born out of the Civil War, is a great contribution
by a very talented woman. During that conflict, the soldiers
used "John Brown's Body Lies A-Moldering in the Grave" as a
marching tune, mostly because of its snappy tempo. Mrs. Howe
often heard this tune, written by John W. Staffe, and prayed
that she might write more suitable words.

With her husband and some friends, she rode just outside
Washington one day to watch the reviewing of some army troops.

During the course of the day, she heard the soldiers singing "John Brown's Body." One of her companions turned to her and asked why she didn't write more suitable words for the tune.

In recounting the story of her song, she remembered that she awakened the next morning before dawn thinking of the tune and framing verses in her mind. She said, "I sprang out of bed and in the dimness found an old stump of a pen, which I remembered using the day before. I scrawled the verses almost without looking at the paper."

When she returned to her home in Boston, she showed the poem to her neighbor, James T. Field, editor of the *Atlantic Monthly*, who was so stirred that he exclaimed, "This should be called 'The Battle Hymn of the Republic.'" He published it in the February 1862 issue of his magazine and gave Julia Ward Howe an honorarium of five dollars.

Her lyrics, sung to Staffe's marching tune, were received with much enthusiasm. When Abraham Lincoln first heard it, he asked that it might be repeated, and so it was widely used during his presidency.

In 1965, it was presented at the funeral of Sir Winston Churchill. In more recent times it was often heard in activities surrounding the tragedies of September 11, 2001. It is a song that crosses all lines when considering the different categories of music.

Julia Ward Howe lived nearly a century and did many wonderful things, for which she is still remembered, but she is most famous for writing "The Battle Hymn of the Republic."

> Mine eyes have seen the glory
> Of the coming of the Lord:
> He is trampling out the vintage
> Where the grapes of wrath are stored;
> He hath loosed the fateful lightning
> Of His terrible swift sword;
> His truth is marching on.

Chorus:
Glory! glory, hallelujah!
Glory! glory, hallelujah!
Glory! glory, hallelujah!
His truth is marching on.

He has sounded forth the trumpet
That shall never sound retreat,
He is sifting out the hearts of men
Before His judgment seat;
O be swift, my soul, to answer Him!
Be jubilant, my feet!
Our God is marching on.

In the beauty of the lilies
Christ was born across the sea,
With the glory in His bosom
That transfigures you and me.
As He died to make men holy,
Let us die to make men free,
While God is marching on.

Reflection

Great people, as the world counts greatness, live and die and are acclaimed for a while, but God continues to march on. The great God we serve, magnified in this song, is not only a God of terrible wrath against those who disobey Him but is also a God of divine justice and unending truth. Isn't it wonderful to know that He sees us, knows all about us, and cares for us?

43

A Song Written During an Epidemic

Shall We Gather at the River?

Revelation 22:1-7

And he showed me a pure river of water of life,
clear as crystal, proceeding out of the throne of God
and of the Lamb.

Robert Lowry entered the ministry upon graduation from Bucknell University in 1854. It was while he was pastoring in Brooklyn at the Hansen Place Baptist Church that he wrote "Shall We Gather at the River?" The writing of this famous song has its origins in incredible human suffering.

On a hot, sultry day in July 1864, Lowry, then thirty-eight, threw himself on a lounge in his home in a state of exhaustion. All over New York City, people were dying. An epidemic had spread through that great metropolis, and Lowry spent much of his time either visiting sick members or conducting funerals. He fell to thinking of future things, of the death all around him, and of the gathering of the saints around God's throne. He began to wonder why so many of the hymn writers had written so much of the "river of death" and so little of the "river of Life." A song began to take form, first as a question, "Shall We Gather at the River?" Then came the answer, "Yes, we'll gather at the River." Soon the words and music were all completed, and it has become so much a favorite among Christians that you find it in almost every hymnal.

Although Dr. Lowry was very gifted and talented as a music composer, he thought of himself only as a preacher of the gospel; hymn writing was an avocation. It is reported that when Lowry was asked what sort of method he used to write his songs, he responded, "I watch my moods, and when anything strikes me, whether words or music, no matter where I am, at home or on the street, I jot it down. My brain is sort of a spinning machine, for there is music running through it all the time." After his hymns were being sung by thousands of Christians, he declared that he felt "a sort of meanness," since he was basically a pastor and didn't really consider himself a composer.

Who hasn't heard "Nothing but the Blood" or "Christ Arose," two of Robert Lowry's more popular compositions? "I Need Thee Every Hour" he cowrote with Annie Sherwood Hawks, one of his church members. The song has made her famous as a hymn writer as well. He wrote a well-known secular song for a temperance movement, "Where Is My Wandering Boy Tonight?"

Dr. Lowry was a kind and generous man who did all he could to encourage others to make the most of their talents. Although he loved preaching, he underestimated his talents. His sermons made an impact for a moment, but his songs have lived on in the hearts of Christians for more than 125 years.

It has been said by some that Dr. Lowry's "Shall We Gather at the River?" is not completely scriptural, because the Bible says that in heaven the river spoken of flows *"out of* the throne of God and of the Lamb" (Revelation 22:1, emphasis added), and not "flowing *by* the throne of God." I have taken the liberty to make a slight change in the lyrics that appear below:

> Shall we gather at the river,
> Where bright angel feet have trod;
> With its crystal tide forever,
> Flowing from the throne of God?

Chorus:
Yes, we'll gather at the river,
The beautiful, the beautiful river,
Gather with the saints at the river
That flows from the throne of God.

Soon we'll reach the shining river,
Soon our pilgrimage will cease,
Soon our happy hearts will quiver
With the melody of peace.

Reflection

Human suffering was not unique to Robert Lowry's day; sin and suffering have reached epidemic proportions in our society today. Yet God has called believers to look ahead and find hope and joy in the fact that there is a better life waiting for us. In fact, God has promised a river of life to all who believe and trust in Him.

44

A Teen's Highest Moment

My Jesus, I Love Thee

1 John 4:17–21

We love him, because he first loved us.

Few songs have crossed into as many different categories of Christian music as "My Jesus, I Love Thee." Two aspects of the song have made it a favorite among those who love Southern Gospel Music: (1) the message of the Cross of Christ, and (2) the depiction of heavenly things.

We were not always quite sure who wrote this musical masterpiece. In more recent years, information has come to the forefront that has led us to the belief that this song was written by a sixteen-year-old Canadian, William Ralph Featherstone (1846–1873). His creation has become a dearly loved hymn.

It was shortly after the conversion of young Featherstone that he penned the poem that has made him notable. His salvation experience in 1862 was so dynamic and meaningful in his life that he turned to recording his encounter with Christ in a poem. He was not content, as you will see later in this story, to let his poem lie undiscovered in some folder tucked away in a drawer.

Some historians have said that William mailed the poem to a relative in Los Angeles, who apparently sent it to England, where it appeared in the *London Hymnbook* published in 1864, just two years following Featherstone's conversion.

A short time later in Boston, Adoniram J. Gordon began the task of compiling a hymnal for Baptist congregations. As compilers often do, he was going through other hymnals, getting ideas and perhaps some songs for use in his hymnbook. As you have already guessed, he discovered "My Jesus, I Love Thee" in one of those books, which happened to be the *London Hymnbook.* He was greatly moved by the lyrics but felt that he could write a more fitting tune. And so he did. The melody that he composed has carried Featherstone's lyrics to every corner of our world.

Several years ago, I came across the story of a young actress who had become an ardent Christian and who treasured "My Jesus, I Love Thee" so much that she memorized the lyrics. She told the leader of the troupe with which she worked that she had become a Christian and the lifestyle of show business was not what she wanted to follow. They were scheduled to go onstage in another production in a very few days. Because all of the publicity had gone out and the director had no other person to do the part, he pleaded with the actress to carry through with just one more performance. She reluctantly agreed to do so.

Immediately following the performance that evening, she stepped quickly to the front of the stage. It became apparent to the audience that she wanted to speak, and so they listened intently. She began:

> My Jesus, I love Thee, I know Thou art mine;
> For Thee all the follies of sin I resign;
> My gracious Redeemer, my Savior art Thou.
> If ever I loved Thee, my Jesus, 'tis now.

She left the stage, never to return to that kind of vocation. The remainder of the hymn is equally as beautiful:

> I love Thee because Thou hast first loved me,
> And purchased my pardon on Calvary's tree;

I love Thee for wearing the thorns on Thy brow:
If ever I loved Thee, my Jesus, 'tis now.

I'll love Thee in life, I will love Thee in death,
And praise Thee as long as Thou lendest me breath;
And say when the death-dew lies cold on my brow,
If ever I loved Thee, my Jesus, 'tis now.

In mansions of glory and endless delight,
I'll ever adore Thee in heaven so bright,
I'll sing with the glittering crown on my brow,
If ever I loved Thee, my Jesus, 'tis now.

When a person becomes a Christian, the Bible declares, "Old things are passed away; behold, all things are become new" (2 Corinthians 5:17). As you and I look back on our lives and reflect on the "horrible pit" from which we have been lifted, we too should have a strong tendency to draw closer to the Savior.

A. J. Gordon was born in New Hampshire on April 19, 1836. He was educated at Brown University and Newton Theological Seminary, and following his ordination at age twenty-seven, he became the pastor of a Baptist church in Jamaica Plains, Massachusetts. He later pastored the Clarendon Street Baptist Church in Boston and passed away in 1895, at the height of his ministry. And yet, the very peak of his ministry might have been in 1864, when he penned the musical setting that has carried "My Jesus, I Love Thee" around the world.

Reflection

This wonderful gospel song outlines for us what our reaction should be when we're reminded of the magnificent gift of God's love and the death of Christ on the cross to pay for our sins. It also assures us that this glorious relationship will carry on into eternity.

45

America's Beloved Gospel Singer

I'd Rather Have Jesus

James 2:1–12

*Hearken, my beloved brethren, Hath not God
chosen the poor of this world rich in faith, and
heirs of the kingdom which he hath promised to
them that love him?*

George Beverly Shea has been known for decades for his
presentations of favorite evangelistic and gospel songs. But he
recently crossed over into the world of Southern Gospel Music,
thanks to two videos, *Billy Graham Music Homecoming*, volumes 1 and 2, in the Gaither Homecoming series. Although
Southern Gospel fans have known and loved George Beverly
Shea, they have been drawn even closer by these videos.

"America's beloved gospel singer" is a title given to George
Beverly Shea that no other contemporary Christian singer has
ever approached. His rich bass voice, coupled with his sincere
Christian attitude, has carried him to the zenith of man's acclaim for gospel soloists. He has been associated with evangelist Billy Graham almost since Mr. Graham came into national
fame.

Mr. Shea's travels have carried him across our nation and to
scores of nations around the world. He has probably sung to
more people face-to-face than any other singer in the history of

the world. To this day, as a very elderly man, George Beverly Shea's songs are blessings to thousands of Christians who still flock to the Graham evangelistic campaigns and who hear him on radio and by recordings.

On February 5, 1961, Billy Graham was in Tampa, Florida, for one of his one-day stops, where he held a mammoth rally at one of the athletic stadiums. Mr. Shea was the soloist for this meeting, and afterward it was my privilege to interview him concerning his song, "I'd Rather Have Jesus." The following is the sum and substance of what he told concerning the song.

"I wrote 'I'd Rather Have Jesus' in 1933. As I sat one evening playing the piano, my mother brought to me a piece of paper on which was written a poem by Rhea Miller. She thought it to be a very wonderful poem and wanted me to read it. She then asked me to try my hand at writing a melody for it. I began to play as a melody came to me. The melody seemed to fit the lyric and so I began to sing and play for the first time 'I'd Rather Have Jesus.'"

Mr. Shea was born in Winchester, Ontario. He had the advantage of good musical training early in life. He was educated at Houghton College. In earlier years Shea had his share of the lucrative offers of this world, but he thoughtfully turned them down to become a singing servant for the Savior.

When the rich voice of George Beverly Shea is but a memory, many happy Christians will still be singing "I'd Rather Have Jesus."

Reflection

According to the teachings of Christ, "I'd Rather Have Jesus" is one of the most difficult songs to sing and really mean it. When we gain the victory over our desire for more and more of what this world has to offer, we have come much closer to real fellowship with the Savior.

46

Capturing the Joys of the Heart

I Need Thee Every Hour

1 Peter 5:1–11

Casting all your care upon him;
for he careth for you.

The famous pastor and hymn writer Robert Lowry joined hands and hearts with one of his parishioners, Annie Sherwood Hawks, to give America and the world one of the great hymns of comfort and devotion.

Annie Sherwood was born in Hoosick, New York, on May 28, 1835. Early in life she developed a love for poetry, even writing some herself while still in grade school. By age fourteen, she was having some of her poems published. She later married Charles Hawks and they were blessed with three children. During her long residence in Brooklyn, New York, she was a member of the Hanson Place Baptist Church, where for eight years Robert Lowry was her pastor.

Here is Annie Hawk's account of the writing of her song, at age thirty-seven:

"I remember well the morning many years ago, when in the midst of the daily cares of my home, I was so filled with the sense of the nearness of the Master. While wondering how one could live without Him either in joy or pain for any period of time, these words, 'I need Thee every hour,' were ushered into my mind—the thought at once taking full possession of me.

"Seating myself by the open window in the balmy air of that bright June day, I took up my pencil and the words were soon committed to paper, almost as they are sung today. It was only by accident, it seemed at the time, that a few months later my pastor, Robert Lowry, set them to music and for the first time they were sung at a Sunday school convention held in Cincinnati, Ohio. Now of course, I can see God's hand in it all. From there they were taken farther West and sung by many thousands of voices before the echo came back to me—thrilling my heart with surprise and gladness.

"For me the hymn was prophetic rather than expressive of my own experiences at the time it was written, and I did not fully understand why it so touched the great throbbing heart of humanity. It was not until long years after, when the shadow of a great loss fell over my way, that I understood something of the comfort in the words I had been permitted to write and give out to others.

"Now when I hear them sung, as I have sometimes by hundreds of voices in chorus, I find it difficult to think they were ever, consciously, my own thoughts or penned by my own hand."

> I need Thee every hour,
> Most gracious Lord.
> No tender voice like Thine
> Can peace afford.
>
> Chorus:
> I need Thee, O I need Thee,
> Every hour I need Thee,
> O bless me now, my Savior,
> I come to Thee.

I need Thee every hour,
Stay Thou nearby;
Temptations lose their pow'r
When Thou art nigh.

I need Thee every hour,
In joy or pain;
Come quickly, and abide,
Or life is vain.

Her song was popularized by Ira B. Sankey in the great D. L. Moody revival crusades.

Dr. Lowry was a graduate of Bucknell University and an honored Baptist pastor in Pennsylvania, New York, and New Jersey. He was a professor of belles lettres at Bucknell and wrote the tunes for many of the popular contemporary hymns of his day. He published "I Need Thee Every Hour" in his songbook, *Royal Diadem*.

Mrs. Hawks passed away at Bennington, Vermont, on January 3, 1918.

Reflection

The nearness of the Savior, on a moment-by-moment basis, is one of His attributes that brings comfort to us as Christians, no matter where we happen to find ourselves.

47

Saved in a Barn in Ireland

Rock of Ages

1 Corinthians 10:1–13

*And did all drink the same spiritual drink: for they
drank of that spiritual Rock that followed them:
and that Rock was Christ.*

𝒜 Living and Dying Prayer for the Holiest Believer in the
World." This was the first title for one of the most loved of all
hymns, "Rock of Ages." Few hymns, if any, have a similar background. It was born out of argumentation, debate, and criti-
cism and first written and published in the *Gospel* magazine in
1776, edited by Augustus Montague Toplady.

Toplady was born in Ireland on November 4, 1740, the son
of Major Richard and Julia Toplady. After the major died during Augustus's infancy, Julia was greatly responsible for her
son's education. As a teenager, he attended a religious service
being held by a lay preacher in a barn at a place called Codymain,
Ireland. Later, in his writings, Toplady referred to the incident
and pondered how God had brought him to Christ in a barn,
with only a few people present, in an out-of-the-way place in
Ireland, in response to a sermon preached by a gentleman who
could scarcely spell his own name.

Toplady was educated at Westminster and at Trinity College
in Dublin. In 1768, he was appointed vicar of Broad Hembury,

Devonshire. Although he was nourished in the established church, he later converted to Methodism. He then became a Calvinist and entered the Anglican ministry as one of the earliest members of the Evangelical Party, which included John Newton, author of "Amazing Grace," and others. Toplady was not a robust individual, and his body held up for only thirty-eight years under the strain of his fiery zeal. It is reported that he died of tuberculosis.

Toplady's theological differences with John Wesley became one of the more interesting episodes in British hymn history. The poem that we now know as "Rock of Ages" was a part of this debate. The battle waged long between these two theologians, even though Wesley had obtained prominence in England and was fifty years Toplady's senior. Augustus Toplady and John Wesley were very strongly opposed to the other's theology but each maintained his Christian character and his love for the other. It seems they both recognized that it is one thing to disagree and quite another to be disagreeable.

It is interesting to know that Toplady published a book of songs and included in it "Jesus, Lover of My Soul," by—you guessed it—John Wesley.

> Rock of Ages, cleft for me,
> Let me hide myself in Thee;
> Let the water and the blood,
> From Thy wounded side which flowed,
> Be of sin the double cure,
> Cleanse me from its guilt and power.
>
> Could my tears forever flow,
> Could my zeal no languor know,
> These for sin could not atone,
> Thou must save and Thou alone,
> In my hand no price I bring,
> Simply to Thy cross I cling.

While I draw this fleeting breath,
When my eyes shall close in death,
When I rise to worlds unknown,
And behold Thee on Thy throne,
Rock of Ages, cleft for me,
Let me hide myself in Thee.

The musical setting most often used was written in 1830 by Thomas Hastings. Hastings was born in Washington, Connecticut, in 1784, the son of a doctor, and grew up as a farm boy, walking six miles to school. In 1823, he became editor of the *Recorder* in Utica, New York. During his life, he also trained choirs and developed religious music. He penned nearly one thousand hymn tunes and six hundred hymn texts. His son, who became president of Union Theological Seminary, said of him, "He was a devout and earnest Christian, a hard student, and resolute worker, not laying aside his pen until three days before his death." Hastings was buried in Greenwood Cemetery in Brooklyn, near Phoebe Knapp, who wrote the musical setting for Fanny Crosby's "Blessed Assurance."

Reflection

"We do not think it strange or preposterous to wear clothes, the materials of which we borrow from other creatures; and why should it be deemed absurd, that we should hide our spiritual shame, by appearing before God in the garment of another—even the righteousness of Christ." —Augustus Toplady

48

She Didn't Want to Be a Flag-Waver

God Bless America

2 Chronicles 7:12–22

If my people, which are called by my name, shall humble themselves, and pray, and seek my face, and turn from their wicked ways; then will I hear from heaven, and will forgive their sin, and will heal their land.

Since the appalling and frightening events of September 11, 2001, life has changed in America. We as a nation give more thought to the safety of our shores, our cities, and our homes. And since that day, one song has for all intents and purposes become our second national anthem: "God Bless America." Most notably, this patriotic song was sung after 9/11 on the steps of the U.S. Capitol by a gathering of senators, and it is now heard regularly during the seventh inning stretch at New York Yankees baseball games at Yankee Stadium. In a sense, our nation's prayer and our rallying cry has become "God Bless America."

During an Armistice Day celebration in 1939, Kate Smith first sang Irving Berlin's song, launching it on its flight across the United States. It is reported that she hesitated at first to include the song in her program, fearing that she might be called a flag-waver. However, she did decide to include it and as a result became famous. The song became one of the most beloved in America.

Irving Berlin was born Israel Baline in eastern Russia on May 11, 1888. As a youngster, Israel was exposed to music, because his father, Moses Baline, was a cantor in the synagogue. The family moved to New York in 1893 to escape the pogroms in Russia.

By 1907, Berlin had published his first song, and in 1911 he wrote his first big, international hit, "Alexander's Ragtime Band." This success followed his days as a singing waiter in a Chinatown cafe in New York City. During the next fifty years, Irving Berlin wrote hundreds of songs, many of which swept across America—songs such as "White Christmas" and "Always." But all of these pale in comparison to his song of thanksgiving and homage to his beloved adopted country, "God Bless America."

We are so blessed to live, laugh, and love in freedom—freedom to enjoy all that our hearts hold dear. This "solemn prayer" for America has already been answered in countless ways and in millions of lives. Just as Berlin proclaimed, we recognize that God has singularly blessed our nation.

From the peaceful Atlantic that bathes our eastern shores to the restless Pacific in the West, from the massive Great Lakes in the north to the winding Rio Grande that borders us to the south; the unique cities and towns that dot our land, the rolling hills, the spacious plains, the majestic mountains, and the colorful deserts all make up what we lovingly call America. More than any nation on earth, we are a diverse population, gathered from the four corners of the world, working together to make America a unique and unparalleled nation.

If you have ever taken a tour of New York Harbor, you have seen "Lady Liberty" come into view. This grand statue was erected just seven years before Irving Berlin's family reached our shores as immigrants. There is no message on any plaque in America that is more often quoted and that has a more solemn and significant intent: "Give me your tired, your poor, your huddled masses yearning to breathe free. . . . Send these, the homeless, tempest-tossed to me." In this message, America offers to share her blessings with people of every hue, nationality, and ethnic origin and invites all to live in this great land of opportunity.

Irving Berlin was not a shallow patriot, and it was evident that the message of his song came directly from his allegiance to this country. He donated millions of dollars in royalties to organizations such as the God Bless America Fund, the Army Emergency Relief Fund, the Boy Scouts of America, and the Girl Scouts of America.

In 1955, President Dwight D. Eisenhower presented Berlin with the Congressional Gold Medal for "God Bless America" and other patriotic songs. President Gerald Ford presented the Presidential Medal of Freedom to Berlin in 1977.

Irving Berlin died in his sleep at his home in New York City on September 22, 1989, at the age of 101.

Reflection

The next time you have an opportunity to sing "God Bless America" make it a meaningful experience as you join others in this patriotic prayer song. Also, make it your daily petition that the Lord will truly bless our nation with guidance from above, and that each of us will love our fellow Americans.

49

She Helped More than Them All

Just As I Am

John 6:29–51

All that the Father giveth me shall come to me; and
him that cometh to me I will in no wise cast out.

*P*robably the most widely used gospel songs in America today are "Just As I Am" and "Amazing Grace." A complete volume could be written relating the wonderful happenings in
connection with the singing of "Just As I Am," which has been
called the world's greatest soul-winning hymn. Many souls have
been influenced by the message of this song to give their hearts
and lives to Christ.

Charlotte Elliott, born in 1789, was a bright young woman in
England. She became quite notable as a portrait painter and a
poet who wrote unusual and humorous verse. She lived a very
happy life until she was thirty, at which time she was stricken
with an illness that left her in a state of great lamentation and
despair. By age thirty-one she was bedridden.

Two years later, in 1822, a Swiss clergyman named Dr. Cesar
Malan made a visit to Brighton, England, Charlotte's hometown. Dr. Malan was invited to the Elliott home where he counseled with Charlotte. He spoke to her of her need to be a
Christian, to which she replied that she did not know how to
find Christ. He told her, "Come to Him just as you are." The

Holy Spirit caused this phrase to strike a very positive note in her, and then and there she made a firm decision to accept Christ into her life as her Savior.

Although her mental condition became brighter, her physical state did not improve. Each year following Dr. Malan's visit, she recognized and celebrated her spiritual birthday, the day she had given her heart and life to Christ.

In 1836, when her brother, H. V. Elliott, was raising funds for St. Mary's Hall in Brighton, a college for the daughters of poor clergymen, Charlotte wanted so much to have some little part but was hindered by reason of her condition. While members of the church were scurrying about making crafts, cookies, and other kinds of baked goods to be used in the fund-raising, she became frustrated with her situation. Everyone seemed able to help but her.

She then decided to write a poem to help others in her same condition. She remembered the words of Dr. Malan, who had talked to her years before, as he said to her, "Come just as you are." She titled her poem, "Him That Cometh to Me I Will in No Wise Cast Out," based on John 6:37.

It is said that the poem was published without her name and was handed to her one day in a leaflet form by her doctor, who did not realize that she was the author. Tears streamed down her face as she read the verses. Copies of the poem were being sold and the money given to St. Mary's Hall. She then realized that she had at last had a part in the building of the school. Her poem had brought in more money than all of the other fund-raising activities combined. Her brother wrote, "In the course of a long ministry, I hoped to have been permitted to see some fruit of my labors; but I feel more has been done by a single hymn of my sister's."

During the whole of her eighty-two years, Charlotte did nothing more important than the penning of the following hymn, which was later titled "Just As I Am."

Just as I am, without one plea,
But that Thy blood was shed for me,
And that Thou bidd'st me come to Thee,
O Lamb of God, I come! I come!

Just as I am, and waiting not,
To rid my soul of one dark blot,
To Thee, whose blood can cleanse each spot
O Lamb of God, I come! I come!

Just as I am, Thou wilt receive,
Wilt welcome, pardon, cleanse, relieve,
Because Thy promise I believe,
O Lamb of God, I come! I come!

I have seen four additional verses, and yet I do not know exactly how many there were originally. Only eternity will reveal the blessings heaped on other lives by this song. Charlotte Elliott probably would have shouted for joy if she could have heard the following story.

During a song in a church service, John B. Gough was asked by a gentleman next to him in the pew what was to be sung. To the orator the questioner was a most shocking sight—a victim of a nervous disease that had left him blind and twisted in body. The poor man joined the congregation in the singing of "Just As I Am." As they came to the words, "Just as I am, poor, wretched, blind," the twisted soul lifted his sightless eyes to heaven and sang with his whole being. Mr. Gough later said, "I have heard the finest strains of orchestra and chorus this world can produce, but I never heard music until I heard that blind man sing 'O Lamb of God, I come! I come!'"

Charlotte Elliott, while enduring great illness, wrote more than 150 hymns, in addition to a number of books. She passed away in her eighty-second year, on September 22, 1871.

Reflection

"Because Thy promise, I believe. . . ." Oh, that we could take God at His Word! Because God is a loving heavenly Father, He makes it as easy as possible for us to come to Christ. It cost Him all that He had, but our part is simple—we need only to trust what Christ did for us on the cross as payment for our sins and accept Him, unconditionally, as Lord of our lives.

50

Washington Is Burning

The Star-Spangled Banner

Psalm 33

*Blessed is the nation whose God is the LORD; and
the people whom he hath chosen for his own
inheritance.*

$\mathcal{S}$ince the events of September 11, 2001, every area of our
society has been more aware of and thankful for the blessings
that we enjoy as Americans. Some of the most patriotic Americans to be found anywhere are Southern Gospel Music fans.
Songs that have become more dear to them include "God Bless
America," "The Battle Hymn of the Republic," and our national anthem, "The Star-Spangled Banner." Southern Gospel
groups are using these patriotic songs in concerts in and around
the season of our Independence Day.

On August 13, 1814, the citizens of Washington, D.C., watched
in horror as their city burned. The White House, the Capitol,
and most of the other government buildings were ablaze. England and the United States were engaged in the War of 1812.

As the British retreated to ships anchored in Chesapeake
Bay, near the mouth of the Potomac River, they took captive
one William Beanes, a prominent physician and friend of Francis
Scott Key, a lawyer and plantation owner. Key then secured
permission from the government to negotiate for the release

of Beanes. Although Key's efforts were successful, he and Beanes were detained overnight on the British ship *Minden*. Their enemies feared they had learned of the British intention to attack Fort McHenry, near Baltimore.

While onboard the ship, Key and his party watched as darkness fell and obscured Fort McHenry, which had a fifty-foot American flag flying overhead. They watched until the last gleaming of the twilight. A raging battle began. Cannon fire, rockets, and flames allowed glimpses of the flag all through the night. As the day dawned "Old Glory" could be seen, still waving. Beanes and Key rejoiced that the fort had stood. Key was so exuberant he grabbed an envelope from his pocket and began to write what his heart was feeling at the time:

> O say! can you see by the dawn's early light,
> What so proudly we hailed at the twilight's last gleaming?
> Whose broad stripes and bright stars through the perilous fight,
> O'er the ramparts we watched were so gallantly streaming.
> And the rockets red glare, the bombs bursting in air,
> Gave proof through the night that our flag was still there,
> O say, does that star-spangled banner yet wave,
> O'er the land of the free and the home of the brave.

Key finished the poem the next day in a Baltimore hotel room, adding several more verses. The original copy is in the Walters Art Gallery in that city. The poem, sung to an English tune known in the United States as "Adams and Liberty," written by John Stafford Smith, became so popular in our country that Congress made it our national anthem in 1931. The flag that flew over Fort McHenry is now on display in the Smithsonian Institution in Washington, D.C.

Francis Scott Key, a devout Christian, believed deeply in liberty and freedom. It is reported that in 1817 he freed the slaves he had inherited from his wealthy father. Before their release, he helped them with family problems, defended them in the courts at no cost, and started Sunday school classes in order for them to be taught the Bible. He did everything in his power to lighten their burdens. He died on January 11, 1843.

Two statues of Francis Scott Key stand in our nation, one over his grave and another in Golden Gate Park in San Francisco. By order of the government, an American flag flies continuously over Key's burial place in Frederick, Maryland.

Many soldiers in Fort McHenry gave their life's blood on that fateful night, that you and I might be free. Today, multiplied thousands of American men and women lie in Flanders fields and in countless other burial places where crosses mark their graves, row on row. They, too, gave their lives for our freedom—freedom to live and work and play without fear of tyranny. What a wonderful blessing, this freedom we enjoy.

Reflection

Who is the author of liberty? Who is the founder of freedom? You and I can never really be free—free from the guilt of our sins—apart from the freedom that Christ purchased with His blood on Calvary's cross. Oh, to be free from guilt, to know that my wrong has been made right; to know that I am free in our nation and free in my soul—before almighty God.

Endnotes

A Brief History of Southern Gospel Music

1. Albert E. Brumley and Sons, "Albert and Goldie Brumley: Biographical Data and Facts," www.brumleymusic.com/bio.html.

Chapter 41: A Great Capacity for Love

1. S. Trevena Jackson. *Fanny Crosby's Story of Ninety-Four Years.* (New York: Fleming H. Revell, 1915), 55.

Song Index

Author/Composer Index